BERLITZ®

KT-382-662

RO/ME

the staff of Berlitz Guides

Berlitz Trademark Reg. U.S. Patent Office and other countries.
Marca Registrada. Library of Congress Catalog Card No. 75-13203.

Printed in Switzerland by Weber S.A., Bienne.

17th edition (1992/1993)

Updated or revised 1991, 1990, 1987, 1986, 1985, 1984, 1983,
1982, 1981, 1979

How best to use this guide

- All the practical information, hints and tips that you will need before or during your trip start on page 103.

- To capture the flavour of the city and its people, turn to the section Rome and the Romans, page 6.

- For a greater understanding of Rome's past, A Brief History, page 12, documents the major events, summed up by a chronological chart on page 21.

- Rome's principal sights and monuments are grouped between pages 22 and 73. There are also chapters on Rome's churches (p. 74) and museums (p. 79), with suggested day trips on pages 83 to 91.

- Those sights which we most highly recommend are pinpointed by the Berlitz traveller symbol.

- A rundown of entertainment possibilities and yearly events is to be found between pages 91 to 93.

- A section on shopping between pages 93 and 95 gives guidance on where to shop and items to look out for.

- Rome's culinary specialities are described between pages 96 to 102, with advice on tipping and meal times.

- If there is anything you can't find instantly, refer to the index at the back of the book, pp. 126–128.

- Finally, a special insert listing a selection of hotels and restaurants will help solve the dilemma of where to stay or eat.

Text: Christina Jackson and Jack Altman
Editor: Adrienne Farrell
Layout: Max Thommen
Photography: cover, pp. 9, 13, 18–19, 44–45, 87, 88–89, 94–95, Daniel Vittet; pp. 2–3, 6, 10, 16, 22–23, 31, 33, 35, 36–37, 38, 40, 43, 52–53, 55, 57, 60–61, PRISMA; pp. 7, 41, 69, Strawberry Media; pp. 47, 48, 65, 76, 77, 81, Herbert Fried; pp. 59, 67, 70–71, 73, 99, 100, Walter Imber.
We would like to thank Don Larrimore, and Francesco Casertano of the E.P.T. in Rome for invaluable assistance.
Cartography: Falk-Verlag, Hamburg; p. 51, Max Thommen

Photos, cover: Trevi Fountain, pp. 2–3 Rome skyline

Contents

Found an error or an omission in this Berlitz Guide? Or a change or new feature we should know about? Our editor would be happy to hear from you, and a postcard would do. Be sure to include your name and address, since in appreciation for a useful suggestion, we'd like to send you a free travel guide.
Although we make every effort to ensure the accuracy of all the information in this book, changes occur incessantly. We cannot therefore take responsibility for facts, prices, addresses and circumstances in general that are constantly subject to alteration.

Rome and the Romans

The Romans take it all for granted. They are used to sipping their *espressos* alongside a Baroque fountain in a piazza designed for chariot races. Each day on their way to work, they pass ruined temples, triumphal arches and aqueducts without so much as a second glance. They find it unsurprising that a Renaissance palace should sprout from an ancient amphitheatre, that the columns of Minerva should support a shrine to the Madonna, or that great basilicas should flower over the bones of martyrs dead nearly 2,000 years. And they toss their cigarette stubs into trash-bins embossed with the SPQR mark of municipal property with scarcely a thought that the initials of *Senatus Populusque Romanus* (the Senate and People of Rome) once adorned the legions' standards and represent one of the oldest democratic slogans in the world.

Yet in their heart of hearts they appreciate, even more than any of the millions of visitors, the marvel that is Rome.

The secret of the city lies in the ineffable blend of the spiritual and the temporal, of art

and architecture, of history, myth and legend, that binds the 27 centuries of the past into one harmonious present. You may deplore the sound and fury of the traffic, the cars triple-banked in the narrow streets and parked in a rising tide up the slopes of the Aventine. But this is a vibrant, living city and capital of a country of 57 million people. It refuses to consider itself just a museum piece or to allow the centre of power and decision to shift to the empty wide avenues and ultramodern ministries of the southern suburb of EUR.

The city fathers do their best to keep key sites as oases of peace. A few steps up from the tumult and you enter the Renaissance tranquillity of the Campidoglio, an enchantment especially at night, when subdued lighting illuminates the gracious façades of Michelangelo. And you can still find respite among the overgrown ruins of the Forum and Palatine, in the gardens of the Caelian Hill or Pincio and in the awed hush of the great churches and museums.

Sprawling on the rolling plain known as the Campagna,

Hot chestnuts to warm winter shoppers at Porta Portese.

about half-way down Italy's boot, Rome straddles the River Tiber as it winds and loops its way through vineyards and olive groves, pasture and scrub to disgorge into the Tyrrhenian Sea some 24 kilometres (15 mi.) to the south-west.

The municipality of Rome extends over 1,507 square kilometres (582 sq. mi.), with a population of 3 million. But the ancient walled city enclosing the seven hills of the historic kernel *(centro storico)* covers only four per cent of that area. Small as it is, it contains some 300 palaces and 280 churches, the ruins of republican and imperial Rome, numerous parks and gardens, the residence of the Italian president, the houses of parliament and government offices, not to mention countless banks, businesses, hotels, shops, restaurants and bars.

It *is* crowded. But the phlegmatic Romans take it all with characteristic good cheer and above all *pazienza* (patience), the local watchword. Nowhere is this more admirably demonstrated than on the buses. As the great orange monsters lurch through the traffic, passengers cling to the nearest available handle, all the time easing their way to the exit doors through the seemingly impenetrable mass of bodies with a *mi scusi*

here and a *permesso* there. Gesticulating constantly, hurling harmlessly barbed insults, religiously staying out of the sun, irreligiously whispering at mass, honking their horns over a football victory, parading in demonstrations, pampering their children, the Romans live and love life to the fullest.

Rome may at first seem chaotic, unmanageable, like the scattered pieces of a jigsaw. But as you explore the labyrinth of narrow cobbled streets on foot, the time will come when you will step out into a sunny piazza or into view of some historic monument and instantly know where you are. Another piece of the puzzle will have fallen neatly into place.

Architecturally speaking, Rome is also something of a jigsaw, an amalgam of different styles representing every phase of its history. The russet and ochre façades, fanciful fountains and exuberant churches are predominantly from the Renaissance and Baroque periods, but built onto— and out of—the ancient and medieval cities. It is said that were they to rebuild the hole in the side of the Colosseum with

All the grace of Classical Rome in a Vestal Virgin's poise.

its original material, many of Rome's beautiful Renaissance palaces would disintegrate.

In its 2,700 years of history, Rome has known unparalleled glory and utter degradation and humiliation. Its armies under Julius Caesar and Augustus went out and conquered an empire, but when the barbarians swarmed through the gates in successive waves, not a single heroic action was recorded. Under the popes, Rome triumphed again as a place of great beauty, source of learning and capital of the arts. The city remains to this day a memorial to its own supreme intellectual and artistic achievements and the inestimable role it played in shaping Western civilization.

As the spiritual and physical centre of the Catholic Church, Rome plays host to a never-ending tide of pilgrims who come to see the pope, visit the basilicas and pay their respects to the early Christian martyrs at the catacombs. Catholic seminaries and colleges have sprouted all over the city. Priests, monks and nuns, robed in every variety of ecclesiastical costume, are an integral part of the Roman scene.

Cars yield to pedestrians in streets around the Corso.

If for nothing else, follow the maxim "When in Rome..." when it comes to observing those excellent Roman institutions, the afternoon siesta and the evening *passeggiata*. In the torpid hours of the early afternoon, a distinct lull falls over the city, as shops and offices close down and the Romans return home for lunch and a rest. Everything comes to life again in the cool of the evening, as what seems to be the entire population of Rome descends into the streets to stroll along the crowded sidewalks, gaze in shop windows, or watch the world go by from pavement cafés or coffee bars. Join them. Then, like them, linger over several courses in a pleasant restaurant or trattoria and savour the hearty delights of Roman cuisine.

Rome wasn't built in a day, nor should it be visited in one. Take your time and allow the atmosphere to seep in slowly. It is not one building or monument that will leave a lasting imprint, it's that impression of the whole which will stay with you long after you have left. And when you do go, there's no need to say goodbye. You don't even need to throw a coin into the Trevi Fountain. Like everyone else you're bound to come back. *Arrivederci, Roma!* **11**

A Brief History

Cherished legend maintains that Rome was founded by Romulus, sired brother Remus by Mars of a Vestal Virgin and abandoned on the Palatine Hill to be suckled by a she-wolf. Historians agree that the site and traditional founding date of 753 B.C. are just about right.

Archaeologists have further established that the site was occupied as early as the Bronze Age (c. 1500 B.C.) and that, by the 8th century B.C., independent villages had sprung up on the Palatine and Aventine hills and soon after on the Esquiline and Quirinal ridges. All proved favourable spots for settlement, since they were easily defensible and lay close to the midstream Isola Tiberina, which facilitated fording of the river.

After conquering their Sabine neighbours, the Romans merged the group of villages into a single city and surrounded it by a defensive wall, while the marshland below the Capitoline Hill was drained and became the Forum. Under the rule of seven kings, the last three Etruscan, Rome began to develop as a powerful force in central Italy.

The Republic

A revolt by Roman nobles in 510 B.C. overthrew the last Etruscan king and established a republic which was to last for the next five centuries. At first the young republic, under the leadership of two patrician consuls, was plagued by confrontations between patrician and plebeian factions. But the plebs put forward their own leaders, the tribunes, to protect their interests, and, thus strengthened internally, Rome began to expand its influence.

In 390 B.C. the Gauls laid siege to the city for seven months, destroying everything except the citadel on the Capitoline Hill. When the Gauls finally left, the hardy citizens set about reconstructing, this time enclosing their city in a wall of huge tufa blocks. For eight centuries, until the barbarians came, no foreign invader was to breach those walls. Rome now spread its control to the whole of Italy, consolidating its hold with six great military roads fanning out from the city—Appia, Latina, Salaria, Flaminia, Aurelia and Cassia. By 250 B.C. the city's population had grown to 100,000.

Victory over Carthage in the hundred years of Punic wars (264–146 B.C.) and conquests in Macedonia, Asia Minor,

Rome's emblem recalls legend of founder Romulus and twin Remus suckled by a she-wolf.

Spain and southern France extended Roman power around the Mediterranean. When Hannibal invaded Italy over the Alps in the Second Punic War, large areas of the peninsula were devastated and peasants sought refuge in Rome, swelling the population.

The acquisition of a largely unsought empire brought new social and economic problems to the Roman people. Unemployment, poor housing and an inadequate public works 13 programme fomented unrest in the city. Violent civil wars shook the republic, which ultimately yielded to dictatorship. Pro-consul Julius Caesar, who had achieved fame by subduing Gaul and Britain, crossed the tiny Rubicon river marking the boundary of his province and marched on Rome to seize power.

The Empire

Caesar's reforms, bypassing the Senate to combat unemployment and ease the tax burden, made dangerous enemies. His assassination on the Ides of March, 44 B.C., led to a bitter civil war and the despotic rule of his adopted son Augustus, who became the first emperor. Under Augustus, the Pax Romana reigned supreme over the far-flung empire. To make Rome a worthy capital, he added fine public buildings, baths, theatres, temples and warehouses, claiming he had "found Rome brick and left it marble". He also organized public services (including the first fire brigade). This was the Golden Age of Roman letters, distinguished by giants such as Horace, Ovid, Livy and Virgil.

In the first centuries of the empire, tens of thousands of foreigners flooded into Rome, among them the first Christians, including St. Peter and St. Paul. As the new religion gained ground, the emperors tried to suppress it by persecution, but the steadfastness of the martyrs only increased its appeal.

Each of Augustus' successors contributed his own embellishment to Rome. After a disastrous fire ravaged the city in A.D. 64, Nero rebuilt it and provided himself with an ostentatious palace, the Domus Aurea (Golden House) on the Esquiline Hill. Hadrian reconstructed the Pantheon, raised a monumental mausoleum for himself (Castel Sant'Angelo) and retired to his magnificent estate at Tivoli.

In the late 1st and 2nd centuries, Rome reached the peak of its grandeur, with a population numbering over a million. Inherent flaws in the imperial system, however, were to weaken the power of the emperors and lead eventually to the downfall of the empire.

After the death of Septimius Severus in 211, 25 emperors— all made and unmade by the armies—reigned in the short space of 74 years. Assassination was more often than not the cause of death. Fire and plague took their toll of the city's population. In 283 the Forum was almost totally destroyed by fire, never to recover its former magnificence.

As a result of a battlefield vision of the Cross, Emperor Constantine converted to Christianity, made it a state religion in 313 and built the first churches and basilicas in Rome. But in 331 he dealt a fatal blow to the empire's unity when he moved the imperial seat to Byzantium (Constantinople). Many of the nobility and wealthy, as well as talented artists and artisans, went with him, a "brain drain" from which the old capital never recovered. Constantine's move effectively split the empire in two.

The Dark and Middle Ages

As the Western Empire declined, the Romans recruited barbarians into the legions to help defend it against other outsiders. But the hired defenders soon joined the attackers, and the weary and disenchanted Roman populace could not summon up the same enthusiasm to defend the city that they had shown in going out to conquer an empire.

Wave after wave came the dreaded barbarians to sack, rape, murder and pillage— Alaric the Visigoth in 410, Attila the Hun, the Vandals and the Ostrogoths. Finally the barbarian chieftain Odovacar forced the last Roman emperor, Romulus Augustulus, to abdicate in 476. The crumbling Western Empire was at an end. (The Eastern or Byzantine Empire continued to prosper until Constantinople was captured by the Ottomans in 1453.)

In the 6th century Justinian reannexed Italy to his Byzantine Empire and codified Roman law as the state's legal system. But, as later Byzantine emperors lost interest, a new power arose out of the chaos in Rome: the Papacy. Pope Leo I (440–461) had already asserted the position of Bishop of Rome as Primate of the Western Church, tracing the succession back to St. Peter; and Pope Gregory the Great had shown statesmanship in 573 in warding off the Lombards, a Germanic tribe already established in the north of Italy. In the 8th century, citing a document, the *Donation of Constantine* (later found to be forged), the popes began to claim political authority over all Italy.

Rome by this time had been reduced to a village, its small population subsisting in the Tiber marsh on the Campus Martius, deserting the seven hills when barbarian invaders cut the imperial aqueducts. Seeking the powerful support

of the Franks, Pope Leo III crowned their king, Charlemagne, ruler of the Holy Roman (in fact mostly Germanic) Empire, in St. Peter's Basilica on Christmas Day, 800. But the pope had in turn to kneel in allegiance, and this exchange of spiritual blessing for military protection laid the seeds of future conflict between popes and emperors.

Over the next 400 years Italy saw invasions by Saracens and Magyars, Saxons and Normans (they sacked Rome in 1084), with papal Rome struggling along as only one of many feudal city-states on the tormented peninsula. The papacy, and with it Rome, was controlled by various powerful families from the landed nobility. As the situation in Rome degenerated into chaos—deplored by Dante in his *Divine Comedy*—the popes moved to comfortable exile in Avignon in 1309, remaining under the protection of the French king for 68 years. Rome was left to the brutal rule of the Orsini and Colonna families. Self-educated visionary Cola di Rienzo headed a popular revolution in 1347 and, styling himself Tribune of Rome, governed for a brief seven months before the nobles drove him out.

The Renaissance

Re-established in Rome in 1377, the popes harshly put down any resistance to their rule and remained dominant in the city for the next 400 years. Yet, during the 15th and 16th centuries, the papacy also became a notable patron of the Renaissance, that remarkable effusion of art and intellectual endeavour which gloriously transformed medieval Rome from a squalid, crumbling and fever-ridden backwater into the foremost city of the Christian world.

It was Giorgio Vasari, facile artist but first-rate chronicler of this cultural explosion, who dubbed it a *rinascita* or rebirth of the glories of Italy's Greco-Roman past. But even more, it proved, with the humanism of Leonardo da Vinci and Michelangelo and the political realism of Machiavelli, to be the birth of our modern age.

True father of Rome's High Renaissance, Pope Julius II (1503–13) began the new St. Peter's, commissioned Michelangelo to paint the ceiling of the Vatican's Sistine Chapel and Raphael to decorate the

Ancient Roman, Renaissance, Baroque and modern—Rome's history permeates Piazza Navona.

17

Stanze. Architect Donato Bramante was nicknamed *maestro ruinante* because of all the ancient monuments he dismantled to make way for the pope's megalomaniac building plans. With the treasures uncovered in the process, Julius founded the Vatican's magnificent collection of ancient sculpture.

The exuberant life of Renaissance Rome was brutally snuffed out in May, 1527, by mutinous troops of the invading German emperor (and Spanish king), Charles V. It was to be the last—and worst—sack of the city.

Counter-Reformation

Meanwhile the position of the papacy and the doctrines of the Church of Rome were being challenged by Luther, Calvin and other leaders of the Protestant Reformation. The Church's Counter-Reformation, formally proclaimed in 1563, reinforced the Holy Office's Inquisition to combat heresy and the Index to censor the arts. Italian Protestants fled and Jews in Rome were shut up in a ghetto.

Art proved a major instrument of Counter-Reformation propaganda. As the Church regained ground, it replaced the pagan influences of Classicism with a more triumphant image,

epitomized by Bernini's grandiose Baroque altar in St. Peter's.

In the 18th century, Spain's authority over many of the states in Italy passed to the Habsburgs of Austria, who were determined to curb the power of the popes in Rome. The papacy lost prestige with the enforced dissolution of the Jesuits and the crippling loss of revenue from the Habsburg church reforms and now sank to its lowest ebb.

In 1798 Napoleon's troops

18

Vittorio Emanuele Monument honours Italy's unity.

entered Rome and later seized the Papal States and proclaimed a republic. They treated old Pius VI with contempt and carried him off a virtual prisoner to France. His successor Pius VII was forced to anoint Napoleon as Emperor and in turn was also made prisoner, returning to Rome only after Napoleon's defeat in 1814. But, during the French occupation, a national self-awareness had begun to develop among Italians, who challenged the re-establishment of Austrian rule.

Many people looked to Pope Pius IX to lead this nationalist movement, but he feared the spread of liberalism and held back. In 1848, when a republic **19** was set up in Rome by Giuseppe Mazzini in the name of Italian nationalism, the pope fled the city. He returned only the following year after the republic had been crushed by the French army.

National unity for most of Italy was achieved in 1860 through the shrewd diplomacy of Cavour, the first prime minister, the heroics of adventurer Giuseppe Garibaldi and the leadership of King Vittorio Emanuele of Piedmont. The nationalists captured Rome in 1870 and made it capital of the Kingdom of Italy the following year. Pope Pius IX retreated to the Vatican and declared himself a "prisoner of the monarchy".

The Modern Era

World War I saw Italy on the winning side against Austria and Germany. But, after the peace conference of 1919, general disarray on the political scene led to an economic crisis, with stagnant productivity, bank closures and rising unemployment. Threatened by the Fascists' March on Rome in 1922, King Vittorio Emanuele III meekly invited their leader, *il Duce* Benito Mussolini, to form a government.

Once firmly established in power, Mussolini made peace with the pope by the Lateran Treaty of 1929, which created a separate Vatican state and perpetuated Catholicism as Italy's national religion. He diverted attention from the worsening economic climate at home with an invasion of Ethiopia in 1936 and proclamation of the Italian Empire. Two years later he introduced German-style racist legislation against Italy's 57,000 Jews. After France's collapse in 1940, Italy plunged on Germany's side into World War II.

The Allies landed in Sicily in June 1943 and fought their way up the peninsula. Rome was declared an open city to spare it from bombing and was liberated in 1944 with its treasures intact. Mussolini was caught fleeing to the Swiss border by Italian partisans and executed.

In June 1946, Italy voted in a referendum to abolish the monarchy and establish a democratic republic. Adherence to the grouping of states which became the European Economic Community opened up wider opportunities for trade and the hope of squeezing some of the benefits of Italy's post-war "economic miracle" down from the north into the more deprived southern half of the mainland and the islands of Sicily and Sardinia.

Historical Landmarks

Earliest Beginnings	753 B.C.	Legendary founding of Rome.
	510	Establishment of Republic.
	390	Gauls sack the city.
	264–146	Punic Wars against Carthage.
	49	Julius Caesar seizes power.
	44	Caesar assassinated in Rome.
Empire	27 B.C.	Augustus becomes first Roman emperor.
	c. 64 A.D.	Persecution of Christians begins.
	312	Constantine turns Christian.
	331	Imperial capital moved to Byzantium.
Dark and Middle Ages	410	Visigoths sack Rome.
	440–461	Leo I asserts papal authority.
	476	End of Western Roman Empire
	800	Pope crowns Charlemagne in St. Peter's.
	1084	Normans sack Rome.
	1309–77	Popes exiled to Avignon.
Renaissance and Counter-Reformation	1508–12	Michelangelo paints Sistine Chapel ceiling.
	1527	Sack of Rome by Imperial troops.
	1798–1809	Napoleon's troops enter Rome, establish republic.
Risorgimento	1814	Pope restored with Austrian rule.
	1848	Italian Nationalists revolt.
	1861	Italy unified.
	1871	Rome capital of Italy.
Modern Era	1915	Italy enters World War I.
	1922	Mussolini begins Fascist regime with March on Rome.
	1929	Lateran Treaty creates separate Vatican state.
	1940	Italy joins Germany in World War II.
	1944	Allies liberate Rome.
	1946	Monarchy abolished in favour of republic.

What to See

Within and beyond its seven hills and along the winding banks of the River Tiber, Rome has four or five different personalities: ancient Rome of the imperial ruins; Catholic Rome of the Vatican and churches; the Renaissance city of Michelangelo and Raphael or the Baroque of Bernini and Borromini; and a modern metropolis of interminable traffic jams, fashionable boutiques and cafés, but also factories and high-rises in the industrial suburbs. None is easily separable from the others. The secret

The Essentials
For those making only a brief visit to Rome, here are the very highest of the highlights:
Roman Forum
Campidoglio
Colosseum
St. Peter's Basilica
Vatican Museums
Spanish Steps
Trevi Fountain
Piazza Navona
Pantheon

Even the tourists desert the Colosseum at siesta time.

of the Eternal City is that it has lived all its ages simultaneously.

But it's a big city and on a first visit, you are well advised to begin with an orientation tour by bus. All large travel agencies conduct daily tours with informative commentaries on major sights by guides who speak a variety of languages. The tours usually last about three hours and can be booked by any hotel desk-clerk.

For the rest, you should see Rome on foot. Virtually all the major sights lie within comfortable walking distance of each other, though you will need several days to cover the most outstanding sights. In this guide, we have grouped together places which can be most conveniently visited on the same walking tour.

A word about opening hours of museums and historic sites: keeping track of all the variations is a nightmare. The best advice we can give is to check at the tourist office, your hotel or in the papers to avoid disappointment. Keep as a general rule of thumb that most museums close on Mondays and that many open only until 1 or 2 p.m. Churches close at midday and reopen in the afternoon. In high season, longer hours are the rule.

Preserving for Posterity

Exposure to weather, earthquakes and fire has scarcely inflicted more damage on Rome's historic and artistic heritage over 2,000 years than the effects of car exhausts over a matter of decades. The level of pollution in the city centre is reckoned to be the highest in Europe. Alarmed, the city has begun an intensive restoration programme, combined with a ban on traffic in sensitive spots.

Piazzas now declared pedestrian-only zones have become havens of peace. Blackened buildings are being systematically cleaned. Ancient columns and statues have disappeared under scaffolding and swathes of green net.

Some museums are closed temporarily, for days, months, even years, for restoration *(restauro)*. This is a blanket term covering budgetary problems, lack of staff or modern security systems or genuine, long-overdue renovation of the building and restoration of the paintings.

Don't be too disappointed if some of Rome's treasures are not visible at the time of your visit. With a little luck, they will be next time.

Modern and Renaissance Rome

The Rome of Michelangelo and Bernini is also the modern Italians' Rome. It grew up on what was, in Roman times, the Campus Martius, lying in a loop in the Tiber. Ironically, today's most crowded quarter was considered uninhabitable by the ancient Romans because of frequent flooding. Lying outside the earlier city walls, the "Field of Mars" was where the legions exercised, ambassadors were received and emperors cremated, and during the republic it became a site of public entertainment. Of the temples, baths, theatres and stadiums, few vestiges remain, and your lingering impression will be of piazzas designed like stage sets, glorious fountains and peach-coloured Renaissance palaces from the heyday of the popes.

Around the Piazza Venezia

Unlike many Italian cities, Rome has no main square as its heart. In Roman times, life centred on the Forum, but as the medieval and then Renaissance city evolved, innumerable piazzas emerged scattered throughout the city, each one laying some claim to eminence.

The nerve centre, at least for traffic, has to be the **Piazza Venezia**. Four major thoroughfares, Via del Corso, Via dei Fori Imperiali, Via Nazionale and Via del Teatro di Marcello converge on this open space dominated by the massive bulk of the **Vittorio Emanuele Monument** (il Vittoriano). Celebrating the first king of unified Italy with inimitable 19th-century pomposity, the dazzling white marble edifice with bombastic colonnade was met with almost universal hostility and derisive nicknames such as the "Wedding Cake" and "Rome's False Teeth". But as a giant landmark, it proves tremendously helpful in finding the way around the city. The nation's Unknown Soldier of World War I lies buried here.

Turn with relief to the early Renaissance **Palazzo Venezia,** termed the finest palace of Christian Rome. Crowned with battlements and pierced by arched windows, the severe but elegant edifice was built for Cardinal Pietro Barbo, later Pope Paul II, supposedly so that he could watch the horse races along the Corso in comfort. Subsequently it served as the embassy of the Republic of Venice and more recently as the private office of Mussolini. His **27** desk stood in the far corner of the vast Sala del Mappamondo to intimidate visitors who had to cross the full length of the marble floor to approach him. A tiny balcony from which *Il Duce* harangued his followers overlooks the square. The palace now contains a museum of medieval and Renaissance arms, furniture, tapestries, ceramics and sculpture.

Two flights of steps lead up from behind the Vittorio Emmanuele Monument. The more gradual and graceful, known as La Cordonata, takes you up between larger-than-life Roman statues of the heavenly twins, Castor and Pollux, to the quiet elegance of the **Campidoglio** atop the Capitoline Hill, once the Capitol and most sacred site of ancient Rome.

Symbolically, Michelangelo's beautifully cambered square turns its back on the Forum and pagan Rome to face the "new" Christian Rome and St. Peter's. A gilt bronze equestrian **statue of Marcus Aurelius** normally graces the centre. The handsome bearded and curly-headed figure escaped destruction over the centuries because it was believed to be Constantine, first Christian emperor. After undergoing prolonged restoration to repair the "bronze can-

cer" corroding its metal, the statue is expected to be replaced by a copy and the original displayed in the Capitoline Museums. At the back of the square stands the 16th-century **Palazzo Senatorio** (now the City Hall).

The Palazzo Nuovo and the Palazzo dei Conservatori, flanking the square, house sections of the **Capitoline Museums.** Gorgeously decorated rooms, with gilt and coffered ceilings and frescoed walls, feature a display of sculpture excavated from ancient Rome. Look out for the poignant statue of the **Dying Gaul** and the beautifully poised bronze of a boy taking a thorn from his foot. In an octagonal recess off the sculpture gallery is the sensual **Capitoline Venus**, a Roman copy of a Greek original dating from the 2nd century B.C. She survives today thanks to a by-gone art-lover who walled her up in a hiding place to preserve her from destruction by early Christians. The museums' most celebrated piece is undoubtedly the **Capitoline She-Wolf**, an Etruscan bronze from the 5th-century B.C., which has become the symbol of Rome. The infant Romulus and Remus that she is suckling are Renaissance additions by Pollaiuolo. The giant

Artists Galore

A host of artists and architects contributed to Rome's splendour. Here are some names that will crop up repeatedly during your visit, with examples of their most famous works in Rome:

Arnolfo di Cambio (c. 1245–1302). Gothic architect and sculptor from Pisa. *Statue of St. Peter in St. Peter's Basilica, tabernacle in St. Paul's.*

Bernini, Gianlorenzo (1598–1680). As painter, sculptor and architect, the foremost exponent of Baroque art. *St. Peter's Square, Fountain of the Four Rivers, Palazzo Barberini . . . the list is endless.*

Borromini, Francesco (1599–1667). Baroque architect, assistant to and later great rival of Bernini. *Sant'Agnese in Agone, Palazzo Barberini.*

Bramante, Donato (1444–1514). Architect and painter from Urbino. Foremost architect of High Renaissance. *St. Peter's, Belvedere Courtyard in the Vatican.*

Canova, Antonio (1757–1822). Most celebrated sculptor of Neoclassical movement. *Statue of Napoleon's sister Pauline in Borghese Gallery.*

Caravaggio, Michelangelo Merisi da (1571–1610). Greatest Italian painter of 16th century. *Crucifixion of St. Peter and Conversion of St. Paul in Santa Maria del Popolo.*

Maderno, Carlo (1556–1629). Architect from northern Italy. *Façade of St. Peter's, pope's palace at Castel Gandolfo.*

Michelangelo Buonarroti (1475–1564). Florentine painter, sculptor and architect, one of the most influential men in history of art. *Dome of St. Peter's Basilica, Pietà, Sistine Chapel ceiling, Moses in San Pietro in Vincoli, Campidoglio.*

Pinturicchio, Bernardino (c.1454–1513). Painter from Perugia. *Frescoes in Sistine Chapel, Borgia Apartments, Santa Maria del Popolo and Santa Maria in Aracoeli.*

Raphael (Raffaello Sanzio, 1483–1520). Painter and architect of High Renaissance. *Stanze in Vatican, Chigi Chapel in Santa Maria del Popolo, La Fornarina in Palazzo Barberini.*

Valadier, Giuseppe (1762–1839). Archaeologist, town-planner and architect for Napoleon. *Piazza del Popolo, Pincio gardens.*

The First Capitol Hill

To the Romans, the Capitol was both citadel and sanctuary, the symbolic centre of government, where the consuls took their oath and where the Republic's coinage was minted. Its name, now applied to many legislatures across the world (notably Congress in Washington), originated in a legend that the skull of a mythical hero was unearthed here during excavations for the temple of Juno. Augurs interpreted this as a sign that Rome would one day be head *(caput)* of the world.

When the Gauls sacked Rome in 390 B.C., the Capitol was saved by the timely cackling of the sanctuary's sacred geese which warned that attackers were scaling the rocks.

Later, victorious Caesars ended their triumphal processions here. They rode up from the Forum in chariots drawn by white steeds to pay homage at the magnificent gilded temple of Jupiter, which dominated the southern summit of the Capitoline.

In the Middle Ages, the collapsed temples were pillaged and the hill was abandoned to goats until Pope Paul III in the 16th century commissioned Michelangelo to give it new glory.

head, hand and foot in one of the courtyards come from a statue of Emperor Constantine. Visit the museums' **Picture Gallery** *(Pinacoteca Capitolina)* for important Venetian works by Bellini, Titian, Tintoretto, Lotto, Veronese and Caravaggio.

Alongside the Palazzo Senatorio, a cobbled road opens onto a terrace which gives you the first glimpse of the ruins of the Roman Forum (p. 49), stretching from the Arch of Septimius Severus to the Arch of Titus, with the Colosseum beyond. Gory detail—from the Tarpeian Rock on your right the Romans hurled traitors to their death.

The steeper flight of steps up the Campidoglio climbs to the austere 13th-century church of **Santa Maria in Aracoeli,** on the site of the great temple of Juno Moneta, where the Tiburtine Sybil announced the coming of Christ to Augustus. The church harbours the curious and much-revered **Bambino,** kept in a separate little chapel. Some Romans attribute miraculous healing powers to this statue of the infant Jesus. Stacks of unopened letters from all over

Harmony reigns in the Piazza del Campidoglio, Rome's quiet heart.

the world addressed to Il Bambino surround the stumpy jewel-bedecked figure. At Christmas it becomes the centrepiece of the manger scene. Pinturicchio's frescoes in the first chapel on the right of the nave recount the story of his namesake St. Bernardino of Siena.

The Corso

This mile-long thoroughfare, more properly the Via del Corso, runs straight as an arrow from the Piazza Venezia to the Piazza del Popolo. It took its name from the wild races of riderless Barbary horses, "Corsa dei Barberi", once the main attraction of the Roman carnival. Most fun at the hour of the evening stroll or *passeggiata*, the street is lined with shops, palaces and churches.

In **Piazza Colonna**, the column of Marcus Aurelius, decorated with spiralling reliefs of the emperor's military triumphs, rises in front of the Italian prime minister's offices in the Chigi Palace. Some 200 steps lead up inside the hollow column to the 16th-century statue of St. Paul at the top, which replaced the original bronze of the philosopher-emperor.

On adjacent **Piazza Montecitorio**, dominated by an Egyptian obelisk from the 6th century B.C., stands the Chamber of Deputies *(Camera dei Deputati)*, Italy's legislative lower house, designed by Bernini as a palace for the Ludovisi family.

Turn off the Corso to the banks of the Tiber, to visit the **Ara Pacis Augustae**, disappointingly boxed in an unprepossessing white and plate glass building. When fragments of this "Altar of Peace", commissioned to celebrate Augustus' victorious campaigns in Gaul and Spain, first came to light in 1568 they were dispersed among several museums, but were returned when reconstruction began. Along the friezes you can make out Augustus himself, with his wife Livia and daughter Julia, friend Agrippa and a host of priests, nobles and dignitaries.

Alongside it, the green mound encircled by cypresses is the **Mausoleum of Augustus,** repository for the ashes of the Caesars until Hadrian built his own mausoleum (now the Castel Sant'Angelo, p. 61) across the Tiber.

At its northern end the Corso culminates in the harmonious curving **Piazza del Popolo**, an exemplary piece of open-air urban theatre designed in 1816 by Giuseppe Valadier, former architect to Napoleon. The cen-

Not even the traffic distracts an ancient Roman from his news.

tral obelisk, dating back to the Egypt of Rameses II (13th century B.C.), was brought to Rome by Augustus and erected in the Circus Maximus. Pope Sixtus V had it moved here in 1589.

The square takes its name from the Renaissance church of **Santa Maria del Popolo**, built on the site of Nero's tomb to exorcize his ghost, reputed to haunt the area. Its interior, remodelled in the Baroque era, is famous for its works of art.

They include an exquisite fresco of the Nativity by Pinturicchio and Raphael's Chigi Chapel, built as a mausoleum for the family of the immensely rich Florentine banker and patron of the arts, Agostino Chigi. In the Cerasi Chapel left of the choir hang two powerful canvases by Caravaggio, the *Conversion of St. Paul* and the *Crucifixion of St. Peter*, notable for the dramatic use of light and shade and the masterly foreshortening of the figures.

Next to the church, the arched 16th-century **Porta del Popolo** marks the gateway to ancient Rome at the end of the 33

Via Flaminia, which led from Rimini on the Adriatic Coast. Pilgrims arriving in Rome by the gate were greeted by the imposing twin Baroque churches of Santa Maria dei Miracoli and Santa Maria in Montesanto, guarding the entrance to the Corso on the south side of the square.

Above the piazza to the east, reached by a monumental complex of terraces, the **Pincio** gardens offer a magical view of the city, especially at sunset, when the rooftops are tinged with purple and gold. Also the work of Valadier, the gardens occupy the site of the 1st-century B.C. villa of Lucullus. This provincial governor returned enriched by the spoils of Asia to impress his contemporaries by his extravagant life style.

The gardens stretch on into the less formal park of the **Villa Borghese**, once the estate of Cardinal Scipione Borghese, nephew of Pope Paul V. The extensive grounds contain the Borghese Gallery (see p. 79) in the cardinal's former palace and a zoo to the north. Lined with pine trees and open-air cafés, the Pincio promenade takes you past the **Villa Medici**, built in 1544 and bought by Napoleon to house the French National Academy.

Around the Piazza di Spagna

At one time Rome's bohemian quarter, the **Piazza di Spagna** is now the heart of the city's most fashionable shopping area, extending over to the Corso.

The boat-shaped marble fountain, **Fontana della Barcaccia,** forever foundering in the centre of the piazza, was designed by the great Bernini's father. From the square, the **Spanish Steps** (*Scalinata della Trinità dei Monti*) ascend grandly in three tiers, with the twin-belfried French church of Trinità dei Monti soaring above. From the top of the steps you have a splendid view across Rome, over myriad roof gardens, dripping with greenery and flowers, which constitute outdoor living-rooms for the fortunate owners of top-floor apartments.

The steps have nothing Spanish about them (other than that the Spanish Embassy to the Holy See stands nearby), but were the idea of a *French* diplomat, Stéphane Gouffier, and realized half a century later in 1721 by the architects Francesco de Sanctis and Ales-

View from the Pincio stretches from Piazza del Popolo across the Tiber to St. Peter's.

sandro Specchi. Now they are the eternal hangout of guitar-playing youths, lovers, hippies and pedlars of trinkets and flowers.

Ordinary tourists and Italians, too, enjoy basking in this pleasant daze, which the poet John Keats celebrated as a "blissful cloud of summer indolence". He should know; the window of the room where he died in 1821 looks out onto the steps. The second floor of his house has been preserved as the **Keats-Shelley Memorial**.

The venerable **Babington's Tea Rooms**, a relic of the days when English lords rolled up in carriages in the 18th and 19th centuries on their grand tour of Europe, offer genteel afternoon tea and hearty American breakfasts.

More quintessentially Roman, on nearby Via Condotti, is the city's oldest coffee house (1760), the **Caffè Greco**. The walls of this mini-museum are covered with autographed portraits, busts and statues, bearing witness to its famous clientele, among them Goethe, Byron, Baudelaire, Liszt, Gogol and Fellini.

Free seats for all on the Spanish Steps to watch the world go by.

The **Trevi Fountain** *(Fontana di Trevi)*, tucked away behind narrow alleys, is an extravaganza out of all proportion to its tiny piazza. Nicola Salvi's astounding 18th-century fountain is in fact a triumphal arch and palace façade (to the old Palazzo Poli), framing mythic **38** creatures in a riot of rocks and

There's still magic in the toss of a coin at Trevi Fountain.

pools. The massive figure of Neptune rides on a sea-shell drawn by sea horses, the rearing steed symbolizing the ocean's turmoil and a calmer one its tranquillity. You may have to compete with the crowds, even late at night when the fountain is illuminated, to throw a coin in over your shoulder and ensure your return to Rome. Urchins think up all manner of devious means to snatch some of the considerable revenues, which are otherwise collected by the municipality of Rome.

The fortress-like **Palazzo del Quirinale** crowns the highest of Rome's original seven hills, once summer residence to popes escaping the malarial swamps of the Vatican down by the Tiber. From this palace, Napoleon's men kidnapped one pope (Pius VI) and arrested another (Pius VII), while a third (Pius IX) fled from revolutionary crowds in 1848. After 1870 it housed the King of Italy and is now the presidential palace.

The piazza, with magnificent statues of Castor and Pollux flanking an ancient obelisk, affords a panoramic view—somewhat marred by the forest of television aerials—over the city towards St. Peter's.

That symbol of the *dolce vita*, the **Via Veneto**, has been more or less deserted by its starlets and *paparazzi*, but the cafés, shops and hotels remain just as expensive.

Around the Piazza Navona

Pause at a café in that serenest of city squares, the **Piazza Navona**. Nowhere in Rome is the spectacle of Italian street life so pleasantly indulged, thanks to an inspired collaboration of Roman genius across the ages. The elongated piazza was laid out around A.D. 90 by Emperor Domitian as an athletics stadium, *Circus Agonalis*—a sporting tradition continued in the Middle Ages with jousting tournaments. The 17th century contributed its sublime décor.

Until 1867 it was the scene of curious water pageants in July and August, when the fountains were allowed to overflow until the piazza was flooded. As bands played, the aristocracy drove through the water in their gilded coaches, to the delight of the onlookers. Today, sages on the city council safeguard it as a pedestrian zone.

Reigning over the square, on a base of craggy rock and topped by an obelisk, Bernini's **Fountain of the Four Rivers** *(Fontana dei Fiumi)* celebrates the world's great rivers, Rio de la Plata (the Americas), Danube (Europe), Ganges (Asia) and Nile (Africa). Romans who delight in Bernini's scorn for his rivals suggest that **39** the Nile god covers his head rather than look at Borromini's church of **Sant'Agnese in Agone** and that the river god of the Americas is shielding himself in case it collapses. In fact the fountain was completed several years *before* Borromini's splendid—and structurally impeccable—façade and dome.

Via dei Coronari, the old Street of the Rosary Makers, is now the Street of Very Expensive Antique Shops. The narrow cobbled lane draws collectors from around the world. Along the street stands the huge and sombre Lancellotti Palace, seat of a great aristocratic family. In 1870, when Italian troops occupied papal Rome, the prince was so angered that he locked his main door, which remained unopened until the 1929 Lateran Pact reconciled Church and State.

The **Pantheon**, in Piazza della Rotonda, stands out as the best preserved monument

of ancient Rome—it was converted into a church in the 7th century—and rivals the Colosseum in its combination of quiet elegance and massive power. Emperor Hadrian, its builder (around A.D. 120), achieved a marvel of engineering with the magnificent coffered dome (larger than St. Peter's), measuring 43 metres (142 ft.) across the interior diameter, exactly equal to its height. With typical modesty, Hadrian left the inscription of the original builder in 27 B.C., Marcus Agrippa, but the stamp on every brick proclaims that it was constructed in the time of Hadrian.

The portico is supported by 16 monolithic pink and grey granite columns. The bronze beams that once adorned the entrance were taken away by

Enduring Bernini statue on the fountain; ephemeral portrait on the pavement.

Pope Urban VIII to make Bernini's canopy for the high altar in St. Peter's. His action prompted the saying: "Quod non fecerunt barbari, fecerunt Barberini." ("What even the barbarians did not do was done by the Barberinis."). A shaft of light illuminates the windowless vault through the circular hole *(oculus)* in the dome, which also (be warned) lets in the rain.

This "Temple of all the Gods" today contains the Renaissance tombs of Raphael and architect Baldassare Peruzzi, and those of modern kings Vittorio Emanuele II and Umberto I. The massive bronze doors remain, but the veneer of precious marbles has long been stripped from the outside walls, and the gilded bronze tiles were carried off by the Byzantine emperor Constans II when he visited Rome in 655.

South of the Piazza Navona, the **Campo de' Fiori** (Field of Flowers) supports a lively and boisterous market, with a jumble of fish, fruit, vegetable, meat and flower stalls, the luscious produce temptingly displayed. In the afternoons, when the stands and brightly coloured awnings have been taken away, political militants hold sway below the statue of the philosopher-monk Giordano Bruno. The Inquisition burned him alive here in 1600 for his preposterous idea that the universe was infinite, with many more galaxies than ours.

An even more famous death occurred at the adjacent Piazza del Biscione. The restaurant Da Pancrazio stands over the foundations of Pompey's Theatre where Julius Caesar was stabbed to death by the conspirators in 44 B.C.

For security reasons, the general public can no longer visit the **Palazzo Farnese**, which has housed the French Embassy since 1871. Antonio da Sangallo the Younger, Michelangelo and Giacomo Della Porta all contributed to this magnificent Renaissance palace, begun in 1515 for Cardinal Alessandro Farnese, later Pope Paul III. Only a privileged few get in to see the ceremonial dining room's fabulous frescoes by Annibale Carracci. The French pay a rent of one lira every year and provide a palace in Paris as Italy's embassy—very nice, too, but not exactly Michelangelo.

Piazza Farnese has been turned into one of Rome's traffic-free squares; at night, the only sound you'll hear is the water splashing into the Egyptian granite basins brought from the Baths of Caracalla for the twin Farnese fountains.

A engineering feat in its time, the Pantheon still amazes with its harmony and durability.

Between the Sant'Angelo Bridge and the Farnese Palace, ancient houses crowd along lanes with intriguing names such as Via dei Cappellari (Street of the Hat-Makers), Via dei Bales-trari (Crossbow-Makers), Via dei Chiavari (Locksmiths) and Via del Pellegrino, along which Holy Year pilgrims used to pass on their way to St. Peter's.

Narrow streets south-east of the Campo de' Fiori take you into the old **Jewish Ghetto**. This district bubbles with life at any time, but particularly so **43** during the evening *passeggiata*. Some of Rome's best restaurants and shopping bargains are found here. Jews were a permanent feature of Roman life for more than 2,500 years but were forced into a ghetto in the 16th century by Pope Paul IV. A small Jewish community still lives around the Via del Portico d'Ottavia. The hefty neo-Babylonian synagogue (1904) down by the river is linked to a museum of Jewish history.

Probably the most captivating fountain in Rome, the 16th-century **Turtle Fountain** *(Fontana delle Tartarughe)* in Piazza Mattei presents a perfect little scene. Four bronze boys perched on dolphins lift four turtles into the marble basin above with gracefully outstretched arms.

A crumbling arched façade more than 2,000 years old, the Portico d'Ottavia, dedicated to Augustus' sister, dominates the ghetto. Beyond extends the

Theatre of Marcellus *(Teatro di Marcello)*, begun by Julius Caesar and architectural model for the Colosseum. The semi-circle of superimposed arches was incorporated into the Palazzo Savelli-Orsini in the 16th century.

The Ponte Fabricio, Rome's oldest bridge (62 B.C.), links the left bank to the **Isola Tiberina**, a tiny island in the river. Three centuries before Christ the island was sacred to Aesculapius, god of healing, to whom a temple and hospital were dedicated. A hospital still stands here to this day, tended by the Brothers of St. John of God. A second bridge, Ponte Cestio, remodelled in the 19th century, leads over to the right bank of the Tiber and Trastevere (see p. 46).

Choosy housewives shop daily for fresh fruit and vegetables in Campo de' Fiori market.

The Aventine

One of Rome's original seven hills, the Aventine remains a quiet sanctuary above the clamour of the city, a favoured residential zone, with villas and apartments set in gardens of flowers and palms.

On the western edge stands the Dominican basilica of **Santa Sabina**, a favourite among the city's many churches for its dignity and purity of line and the grace of its Roman columns. It was built on the site of the palace of a Roman matron, who was converted to Christianity by her Greek slave and martyred in the time of Hadrian. The beautifully carved old cypress-wood doors in the portico are protected from vandalism and graffiti by glass. Through a circular window opposite them **45** you can see the descendant of an orange tree planted by St. Dominic 700 years ago.

A few steps away, take a peep through the **keyhole** in the garden door of the Villa of the Knights of Malta *(Cavalieri di Malta)*, for an unusual view in the distance of the dome of St. Peter's, perfectly framed at the end of an avenue of trees. When busloads arrive, you may have to queue for a look!

Lying at the foot of the Aventine near the Tiber, **Santa Maria in Cosmedin** is a jewel of a church serving Rome's Greek community. Its Romanesque exterior and unadorned interior favour a devout simplicity, in contrast to the Baroque grandeur of many of Rome's churches. The portico contains an ancient marble carving of a fierce face known as the **Bocca della Verità** (Mouth of Truth), possibly once a well cover. Pilgrims of the Middle Ages believed that anyone who told a lie with his hand in the gaping mouth would have his fingers bitten off. Copies of all sizes are on sale at the church.

On the opposite side of the road, two of Rome's most charming and well-preserved temples grace an open green space by the Tiber, once part of the city's ancient cattle-market. The circular marble temple with fluted columns, known erroneously as the **Temple of Vesta** because of its resemblance to the one in the Forum, was probably dedicated to Hercules. Next to it, the rectangular so-called **Temple of Fortune** is now believed to be that of Portunus, god of harbours.

Glance over the Tiber embankment here to see the mouth of the Cloaca Maxima, ancient Rome's main drain, still opening into the river near the Palatine Bridge.

South of the Aventine, near the Porta San Paolo, you should visit the serenely beautiful **Protestant Cemetery**, where Keats lies buried (see p. 37) and Shelley's ashes are interred. Rome's only pyramid, incorporated into the city walls, towers over the cemetery. A Roman praetor, Caius Cestius, commissioned it for his tomb in 12 B.C. on his return from a spell of duty in Egypt.

Trastevere

A crowded, noisy and cheerful neighbourhood south of the Vatican, Trastevere (literally "across the Tiber") has long been renowned as the most popular quarter of Rome. Here, ordinary people—who like the cockneys of London consider themselves to be de-

Will those turtles in Piazza Mattei ever reach the water?

scendants of the original citizens—uphold ancient traditions and customs. Make a point of wandering through the narrow cobbled streets, past quaint tumbledown houses with flowered balconies, to take the pulse of the authentic life of the city, highlighted by the July *Noiantri* ("We Others") street festival of music and fireworks down by the river.

Inevitably, "popular" and "authentic" became chic, and the ambience is now somewhat diluted by a certain smart set moving in—and raising the rents. But the true Trasteverini hang on, mainly in the area immediately around **Santa Maria in Trastevere**, one of the oldest churches in the city. Its foundation (on the spot where oil is said to have gushed to presage the birth of Christ) may date **47**

back to the 3rd century, but the present structure is the work of Pope Innocent II, himself a Trasteverino, around 1140. A wonderful Byzantine-influenced mosaic of Mary enthroned with Jesus decorates the domed ceiling of the apse. The façade's gilded mosaics and the square's gently playing fountain are illuminated at night, providing a perfect backdrop to a meal in one of the restaurants and bars around the square.

Santa Maria in Trastevere's square comes to life at night.

Before entering the church of **Santa Cecilia in Trastevere**, pause in the courtyard to admire the russet Baroque façade and endearingly leaning Romanesque tower. The main altar encloses the serene marble sculpture of St. Cecilia as she lay in her coffin, her body undecomposed, when the sculptor Stefano Maderno saw her in

1599. To the right of the nave is her chapel, over the site of the Roman *caldarium* where this patron saint of music was imprisoned and tortured by scalding. You pay to go down into the crypt, a warren of vaulted rooms and passageways with fragments of old Roman columns and the sarcophagus of St. Cecilia.

Classical Rome

The nucleus of Classical Rome lies around the Colosseum, with the Forum to the northwest and the Baths of Caracalla to the south. Don't be daunted—even the best-informed scholars find the monumental relics hard to decipher. The mystery itself is half the charm of these vestiges of a vanished world. Even if you're not an archaeology buff who wants to understand the meaning of every stone, it's worth at least an hour or two to dream among the debris of empire and wonder whether Fifth Avenue, Piccadilly, the Champs-Elysées or Red Square will look any better 2,000 years from now.

The Roman Forum
(Foro Romano)
With an exhilarating leap of the imagination, you can stand

The Seven Hills
The original Seven Hills of Republican Rome were:

Palatine: Cradle of the city, once covered by palaces, now a garden of ruins.

Capitoline: Ancient citadel, remodelled as Renaissance square by Michelangelo.

Esquiline: Once Sabine stronghold, site of Nero's Golden House on southern crest, dominated by basilica of Santa Maria Maggiore in north.

Caelian: Area of patrician homes, now occupied by ruins, gardens and churches.

Quirinal: Highest of the Seven Hills, crowned by residence of president, once palace of popes and kings.

Viminal: Built-up area near Diocletian's Baths.

Aventine: In imperial times, and still, a smart residential quarter.

among the columns, arches and porticoes of the Roman Forum and picture the hub of the great imperial city, the first in Europe to house a million inhabitants.

Ringed by the Palatine, Capitoline and Esquiline hills and drained by an underground channel, the Cloaca Maxima, the flat valley of the Forum developed as the civic, commer- 49 cial and religious centre of the growing city. Under the emperors, it attained unprecedented splendour, the white marble and golden roofs of temples, law courts and market halls glittering in the sun. After the barbarian invasions, the area was abandoned. Earthquake, fire, flood and the plunder of barbarians and Renaissance architects reduced it to a muddy cow pasture until excavations in the 19th century brought many of the ancient edifices again to light. But grass still grows between the cracked paving stones of the Sacred Way, poppies bloom among the piles of toppled marble, and tangles of red roses entwine the brick columns, softening the harshness of the ruins.

Portable sound-guides are available for hire at the entrance (on Via dei Fori Imperiali) or you can find your own way round the Forum. But first sit down on a chunk of fallen marble in the midst of the ruins and orient yourself with the help of a detailed plan, to trace the layout of the buildings and make sense of the apparent confusion.

Start your tour at the western end, just below the Campidoglio's Palazzo Senatorio (see p. 28). Here you can look up and see how the arches of the

Roman record office *(Tabularium)* have been incorporated into the rear of the Renaissance palace. And from here you can look down the full length of the **Sacra Via** (Sacred Way), along which the victorious generals rode in triumphal procession—followed by the standards of the legions, the massed ranks of prisoners and carts piled with the spoils of conquest—to the foot of the Capitoline Hill.

Then, to counterbalance this image of the Romans as ruthless military conquerors, turn to the severe brick-built rectangular **Curia** (Senate House) in the north-west corner of the Forum. Here you can gaze through the bronze doors (copies of the originals which are now in St. John Lateran, see p. 75) at the "venerable great-grandmother of all parliaments", where the senators, robed in simple white togas, argued the affairs of Republic and Empire. It is worth remembering that the tenets of Roman law, which underpin most western legal systems, were first debated in this modest chamber.

Believed to mark the site of the very first assembly hall of the Roman elders, the Curia was constructed in its present form by Diocletian in A.D. 303 and once faced with marble.

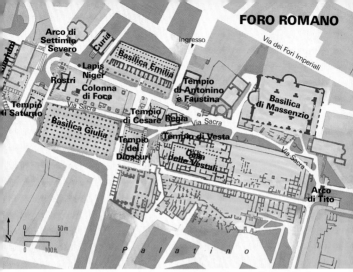

The church that covered it was dismantled in 1937 to reveal the ancient floor set with geometrical patterns in red and green marble, the tiers on either side where the Roman senators sat, and the brick base of the golden statue of Victory at the rear. The Curia shelters two large basreliefs, possibly from the Rostra, outlining in marble the ancient buildings of the Forum.

In front of the Curia, a concrete shelter protects the underground site of the **Lapis Niger** (generally not on view), a black marble paving stone over the traditional grave of Romulus, founder of the city. Beside it, a broken stele engraved with the oldest Latin inscription ever found, dates back some six centuries before Christ; no one has completely deciphered it yet.

The triple **Arch of Septimius Severus** *(Arco di Settimio Severo)* dominates this end of the Forum, depicting the military triumphs in the east of the 3rd-century emperor who later campaigned as far as Scotland and died in York. Nearby, the broad orators' platform or **Rostra**, from which Cicero and Mark Antony harangued the crowds, stretches across the Forum. Its name comes from the iron prows *(rostra)* which once adorned it, taken from the **51** enemy ships at the Battle of Antium in 338 B.C. Two points at each end of the Rostra have special significance: the Umbilicus Urbis Romae, marking the traditional centre of Rome; and the Miliarium Aureum (Golden Milestone), which once recorded in gold letters the distances in miles from Rome to the provinces of the empire.

In front of the Rostra, public meetings and ceremonies took place in the social forum, kept bare save for samples of three plants essential to Mediterranean prosperity—the vine, the olive and the fig. Still prominent above this open space is the **Column of Phocas** *(Colonna di Foca)*, built to honour the Byzantine emperor who presented the Pantheon to Pope Boniface IV.

Eight tall columns standing on a podium at the foot of the Capitol belong to the **Temple of Saturn** *(Tempio di Saturno)*, one of the earliest temples in Rome. It doubled as state treasury and centre of the merry December debauchery known as the Saturnalia, pagan precursor of Christmas.

Of the **Basilica Julia**, once the busy law courts, only the

Broken temple columns line the
Forum's ancient Sacred Way.

paving and some of the arches and travertine pillars survive. Even less remains of the Basilica Aemilia on the opposite side of the Sacra Via, destroyed by the Goths in A.D. 410.

Three slender columns, the podium and a portion of the entablature denote the **Temple of Castor and Pollux** *(Tempio dei Dioscuri)*. It was dedicated to these twin sons of Jupiter (the Dioscuri) after they appeared on the battlefield at Lake Regillus to rally the Romans against the Latins and Etruscans.

You'll have to look for the **altar of Julius Caesar**, tucked away in a semicircular recess of the Temple of the Divine Julius *(Tempio di Cesare)*. On March 19, 44 B.C., the grieving crowds, following Caesar's funeral procession to the cremation spot in the Campus Martius, made an impromptu pyre of chairs and tables and burned the body here in the Forum.

Pause for a pleasant idyll in the **Hall of the Vestal Virgins** *(Casa delle Vestali)*, surrounded by graceful statues in the serene setting of a rose garden and old rectangular fountain basins, once more filled with water. In the circular white marble **Temple of Vesta** *(Tempio di Vesta)*, the sacred flame perpetuating the Roman state was tended by six Vestal Virgins who, from childhood, observed a 30-year vow of chastity on pain of being buried alive if they broke it. They were under the supervision of the high priest, the Pontifex Maximus (the popes have appropriated this title). His official residence was in the nearby Regia, of which only overgrown brick vestiges remain.

Further along the Sacra Via, the imposing **Temple of Antoninus and Faustina** has survived because, like the Curia, it was converted to a church, acquiring a Baroque façade in 1602.

Few ancient buildings reach the massive proportions of the **Basilica of Maxentius**, completed by Constantine (whose name it also bears), of which three giant vaults still stand.

The Sacra Via culminates in the **Arch of Titus**, built to commemorate the sack of Jerusalem in A.D. 70. Restored by Giuseppe Valadier in 1821, it shows in magnificently carved relief the triumphal procession of the emperor bearing the spoils of Jerusalem, among them the temple's seven-branched golden candlestick and silver trumpets which later vanished, possibly in the sack of Rome by the Vandals. Even today, many Jews will avoid walking through the arch, built to glorify their tragedy.

From this end of the Forum, a slope leads up to the **Palatine Hill**, Rome's legendary birthplace and today its most romantic garden. At the time of the Republic, this was a desirable residential district for the wealthy and aristocratic; Cicero and Crassus were among its distinguished inhabitants. Augustus began the imperial trend, and later emperors added and expanded, each vying to outdo the last in magnificence and luxury, until the whole was one immense palace (the very word takes its name from the hill). From the pavilions and terraces of the botanical gardens laid out up here by the 16th-century Farnese family, you have an excellent view of the whole Forum.

The so-called **House of Livia** is now reckoned to be that of her husband, Emperor Augustus, where he lived in characteristic modesty, but good taste. Small but graceful rooms retain remnants of the mosaic floors and a well-preserved wall

Roses bloom again in the Hall of the Vestal Virgins.

painting depicting the love of Zeus for a young priestess. Nearby, a circular Iron-Age dwelling characteristic of the time of Rome's legendary beginnings (see p. 12) is known as **Romulus' Hut**.

Through the Palatine threads the **Cryptoporticus of Nero**, an underground passageway linking the palaces. In the dim light you can make out stucco decorations on the ceilings and walls.

The vast assemblage of ruins of the Domus Flavia include a basilica, throne room, banqueting hall, baths, porticoes and a fountain in the form of a maze. Together with the Domus Augustana alongside, the complex is known as the **Palace of Domitian**. From one side of it you can look down into the **Stadium of Domitian**, more of a vast exercise yard for the imperial family than a ground for public athletics.

Last emperor to build on the Palatine, Septimius Severus carried the imperial palace to the very south-eastern end of the hill, so that his seven-storied **Domus Severiana** was the impressive first glimpse of the capital for new arrivals. It was dismantled to build Renaissance Rome, and only the huge arcaded foundations remain.

From this edge of the Palatine you have a splendid view down onto the immense grassy stretch of the **Circus Maximus,** where crowds of up to 200,000 watched the chariot races from tiers of marble seats. Beyond lies the Aventine Hill (see p. 45).

The separate **Imperial Forums**, along the Via dei Fori Imperiali, were built as an adjunct to the Roman Forum as the capital grew ever larger and were named after Julius Caesar, Augustus, Trajan, Vespasian and Nerva. Most impressive monument is the 30-metre-high (98-ft.) **Trajan's Column** (A.D. 113). Celebrating Trajan's campaigns against the Dacians in what is today Rumania, the minutely detailed friezes spiralling around the column constitute a veritable textbook of Roman warfare, featuring embarkation on ships, the clash of armies and the surrender of barbarian chieftains. St. Peter's statue replaced the emperor's in 1587.

The Colosseum

It says something about Rome's essential earthiness that, more than any inspira-

Time—and man—have gutted the Colosseum.

tional church or opulent palace, it's the Colosseum —what Byron called "the gladiator's bloody circus"— that is the symbol of the city's eternity. Built in A.D. 80 by 20,000 slaves and prisoners, the four-tiered elliptical amphitheatre seated 50,000 spectators on stone benches according to social status. Flowing in and out of arched passageways, nobles and plebs alike came to see blood: bears, lions, tigers and leopards starved into fighting each other and against criminals and, tradition holds, Christians. Gladiators butchered one another to the cries of *Jugula!* ("Slit his throat!"). In one spectacle in A.D. 249, 2,000 gladiators took part and 32 elephants, 60 lions, 10 tigers and 10 giraffes were slaughtered.

For their churches and palaces, popes and princes have stripped the Colosseum of its precious marble, travertine and metal. They have left in the arena's basin a ruined maze of cells and corridors that funnelled man and beast to the slaughter. The horror has disappeared beneath the moss, and what remains is the thrill of the monument's endurance. As an old Anglo-Saxon prophecy goes: "While stands the Colosseum, Rome shall stand; when falls the Colosseum, Rome shall fall; and when Rome falls, with it shall fall the world."

The nearby **Arch of Constantine** honours the ruler's 4th-century battlefield conversion to Christianity and victory over the rival emperor Maxentius at Ponte Milvio north of Rome. Unperturbed by the depiction of pagan rituals and sacrifices, a cost-conscious Senate took fragments from monuments of earlier rulers. Only a few reliefs show the newly Christian Constantine.

A kilometre (half a mile) south of the Colosseum, the huge 3rd-century **Baths of Caracalla** *(Terme di Caracalla)* provided room for 1,600 people to bathe in style and luxury. Imagine the still impressive brick walls covered in coloured marble. The baths and gymnasia were of alabaster and granite, profusely decorated with statues and frescoes. Public bathing was a prolonged social event, as merchants and senators passed from the *caldarium* hot room to cool down in the *tepidarium* and *frigidarium*. The baths ran dry in the 6th century, when barbarians cut the aqueducts. Now the stage for spectacular open-air operas in summer, the *caldarium* is vast enough for processions of elephants, camels and four-horse chariots.

The Vatican

The power of Rome endures in the spirituality evoked by every stone of St. Peter's Basilica and in the almost physical awe inspired by the splendours of the Vatican Palace. At their best, the popes and cardinals replaced military conquest by moral leadership and persuasion; at their worst, they could show the same hunger for political power and worldly wealth as any Caesar. A visit to the Vatican is an object lesson for faithful and sceptic alike.

Constantine, first Christian emperor, erected the original St. Peter's Basilica near (probably over) the site of the Apostle's tomb in A.D. 324. After it was sacked in 846 by marauding Saracens, Pope Leo IV ordered massive walls built around the sacred church, and

A present for the pope?

the enclosed area became known as the Leonine City—later as the Vatican City, after the Etruscan name of its hill.

The Vatican has been a papal residence for more than 600 years, but a sovereign state independent of Italy only since the Lateran Pact signed with Mussolini in 1929. Since 1506, the pope has been guarded by an elite corps of Swiss Guards whose old-style blue, scarlet and orange uniforms are said to have been designed by Michelangelo. The papal domain is served by an independent Vatican radio, a tiny railway station (rarely used) and a separate post office issuing its own stamps, which have become collector's items. Apart from the 440,000 square metres (less than half a square mile) comprising St. Peter's Square, St. Peter's Basilica and the papal palace and gardens, the Vatican has jurisdiction over several extraterritorial enclaves, including the basilicas of Santa Maria Maggiore, St. John Lateran and St. Paul, as well as the Pope's summer residence outside Rome at Castel Gandolfo.

You won't need a passport to cross the border; you will hardly even notice when you do—though it is marked by a band of white travertine stones

Castel Sant'Angelo was in turn tomb, fort, palace and prison.

running from the ends of the two colonnades at the rim of St. Peter's Square. But for a public papal audience, security men will check your bags for weapons before allowing you past the control barriers.

The Vatican Pilgrim and

Tourist Information Bureau on St. Peter's Square arranges guided tours and issues tickets to the grounds of the Vatican City, including the gardens. From here also buses leave regularly to the entrance of the Vatican Museums.

A visit to St. Peter's ideally combines with a tour of the Castel Sant'Angelo, culminating in a picnic and siesta on the nearby Janiculum Hill. It is best to save the Vatican Museums for a separate day.

Castel Sant'Angelo

Cross the Tiber from the left bank by the pedestrians-only **Ponte Sant'Angelo**, incorporating arches of Hadrian's original bridge, the Pons Aelius. The balustrades are adorned by ten windswept angels designed by Bernini, each bearing a symbol of the Passion of Christ.

From the bridge you have the best view of the cylindrical bulk of the Castel Sant'Angelo, its mighty brick walls stripped of **61**

Oh, Tiber! Father Tiber!

The muddy yellow Tiber rolls through Rome almost unobserved, sunk below its high embankments. In imperial times, barges carried obelisks from Egypt and marble from Tuscany right into the heart of Rome. Nowadays, only a few floating restaurants and sunbathing barges lie moored to the banks.

Twenty-six bridges link Renaissance, Classical and business Rome with the Vatican City, Janiculum and Trastevere.

In the early days of the republic, a single wooden bridge straddled the Tiber. When the Etruscans tried to capture the city, the Roman hero Horatius held back an entire army on the narrow bridge, while his fellow citizens cut down the timbers behind him. As the last plank fell, Horatius leaped fully armed into the raging flood and swam safely to the Roman shore, crying (as every schoolchild, with a little help from poet Macaulay, used to know):

> *Oh, Tiber! Father Tiber!*
> *To whom the Romans pray,*
> *A Roman's life, a Roman's arms*
> *Take thou in hand this day!*

Modern Romans can hardly emulate him. Swimming is out because of pollution.

their travertine and pitted by cannonballs, but nevertheless well withstanding the onslaught of time. Conceived by Hadrian around A.D. 130 as a mausoleum for himself and his family, it became part of the defensive Aurelian Wall a century later. It gained its present name in 590 after Pope Gregory the Great had a vision of the Archangel Michael alighting on one of the turrets and sheathing his sword to signal the end of a plague. It remained for centuries Rome's mightiest military bastion and hideout of popes in times of trouble; Clement VII holed up here during the sack of Rome by Habsburg troops in 1527. Here also were kept the Vatican's most precious possessions in treasure chests, still on view.

A spiral ramp, showing traces of the original black and white mosaic paving, leads up to the funerary chamber where the imperial ashes were kept in urns. You emerge into daylight in the **Court of the Angel** *(Cortile dell'Angelo* or *d'Onore)*, stacked with neat piles of cannonballs and watched over by a marble angel. A museum of arms and armour opens off the courtyard.

After the grimness of the exterior, it comes as a surprise

to step into the luxurious surroundings of the old **Papal Apartments**. At times effectively besieged in this fortress, the popes saw to it that they did not lack comforts. Lavish frescoes cover the walls and ceilings of rooms hung with masterpieces by Dosso Dossi, Nicolas Poussin and Lorenzo Lotto. Set away by itself off the Courtyard of Alexander VI is possibly the most exquisite **bathroom** in history. The tiny room, just wide enough for the marble bathtub at the far end, is painted with delicate designs over every inch of its walls and along the side of the bath.

A harsh jolt brings you back to reality as you enter the **dungeons,** scene of torture and executions. You have to bend double to pass through low doors into bare stone cells where famous prisoners languished—among them philosopher Giordano Bruno and sculptor-goldsmith Benvenuto Cellini.

The **Gallery of Pius IV,** surrounding the entire building, affords tremendous views in every direction, as does the terrace on the summit, at the foot of the 18th-century bronze **statue of St. Michael** by Verschaffelt. You may be suitably awed by the thought that this is the stage for the final act of Puccini's opera *Tosca*, in which the heroine hurls herself to her death from the battlements.

St. Peter's

From the Castel Sant'Angelo, a wide straight avenue, **Via della Conciliazione,** leads triumphantly up to St. Peter's. A maze of higgledy-piggledy streets, in which stood Raphael's studio, was destroyed in the 1930s to provide an unobstructed view of St. Peter's all the way from the banks of the Tiber. A thick wall running parallel to the avenue conceals a passageway *(il Passetto)* linking the Vatican to the Castel Sant'Angelo, by which the fleeing popes reached their bastion in safety.

In **St. Peter's Square** *(Piazza San Pietro),* his greatest creation, Bernini has performed one of the world's most exciting pieces of architectural orchestration. The sweeping curves of the colonnades reach out to Rome and the whole world, *urbi et orbi,* to draw the flood of pilgrims into the bosom of the church beyond. On Easter Sunday as many as 300,000 people cram into the space. The square is on or near the site of Nero's circus where many early Christians were martyred.

Bernini completed the 284 **63**

Seeing the Pope

When he's not in Bogotà or Bangkok, it is possible to see the pope in person at the Vatican. He normally holds a public audience every Wednesday at 11 a.m. (5 p.m. in summer). An invitation to the Papal Audience Hall may be obtained from the Pontifical Prefect's Office (open Tuesday and Wednesday mornings) through the bronze gates off St. Peter's Square. A visitor's bishop at home can arrange a private audience.

On Sundays at noon, the pope appears at the window of his apartments in the Apostolic Palace (right of the basilica, overlooking the square), delivers a brief homily, says the Angelus and blesses the crowd below. On a few major holy days, the pontiff celebrates high mass in St. Peter's.

travertine columns and 88 pilasters topped by 140 statues of the saints in just 11 years, from 1656 to 1667. In the centre of the ellipse rises a red granite obelisk (84 feet, 25.5 m. high) brought here from Egypt by Caligula in A.D. 37. Stand on one of two circular paving stones set between the obelisk and the square's twin 17th-century fountains to see the quadruple rows of perfectly aligned

Doric columns appear magically as one. Above the northern colonnade are the windows of the Apostolic Palace where the pope lives and works.

By any standards a grandiose achievement, **St. Peter's Basilica** *(Basilica di San Pietro)* inevitably suffers from the competing visions of all the architects called in to collaborate— Bramante, Giuliano da Sangallo, Raphael, Baldassare Peruzzi, Michelangelo, Giacomo Della Porta, Domenico Fontana and Carlo Maderno, each adding, subtracting, modifying, often with a pope looking over his shoulder.

From 1506 when the new basilica was begun under Julius II to 1626 when it was consecrated, it changed form several times. It started as a simple Greek cross, with four arms of equal length (favoured by Bramante and Michelangelo) and ended as Maderno's Latin cross extended by a long nave, as demanded by the popes of the Counter-Reformation. One result is that Maderno's porticoed façade and nave obstruct a clear view of Michelangelo's dome from the square.

Entering the basilica, you are less inspired by religious fervour than by awe at its magnificence and immensity—it is, after all, the world's largest

Catholic church, 212 metres (695 ft.) in exterior length, 187 metres (613 ft.) long on the inside; 132.5 metres (435 ft.) to the tip of the dome (the dimensions of "lesser" churches such as St. Paul's in London are marked out on the floor of the central aisle).

Set in the floor by the centre door is the large round slab of red porphyry where Charlemagne knelt for his coronation as Holy Roman Emperor (see p. 17).

Crowds throng St. Peter's Square for the pope's blessing.

To the right of the entrance doors, in its own chapel, you'll find the basilica's most treasured work of art, Michelangelo's sublime **Pietà**—Mary with the dead Jesus in her lap—sculpted when the artist was only 25. The life-size figures express with the utmost simplicity the grieving mother's profound love for her son. This is the only one of his sculptures that Michelangelo signed, his name clearly visible on Mary's sash. Since it was attacked by a religious fanatic with a hammer, it has been protected by bullet-proof glass.

Reverence can cause damage, too: on the 13th-century bronze seated **statue of St. Peter,** attributed to Florentine architect-sculptor Arnolfo di Cambio, the toes have been worn away by the lips of countless pilgrims.

Beneath the dome, Bernini's great **baldacchino** (canopy) soars above the high altar, at which only the pope celebrates mass. The canopy and four spiralling columns were cast from bronze beams taken from the Pantheon. Notice at the bottom of each column the coat of arms bearing the three bees of the Barberini Pope Urban VIII who commissioned the work.

In the apse beyond, Bernini

gives full vent to his exuberance with his bronze and marble **Cathedra of St. Peter,** throne of the Apostle's successors, into which is supposedly incorporated the wooden chair of St. Peter.

For his imposing **dome,** Michelangelo drew inspiration from the Pantheon and the cathedral in Florence. A lift will take you as far as the gallery above the nave. From here you have a dizzying view down into the interior of the basilica, as well as close-ups of the inside of the dome. Spiral stairs and ramps lead on and up to the outdoor balcony which circles the top of the dome for stunning views of the Vatican City and all Rome.

The **Vatican Grottoes** beneath the basilica harbour numerous little chapels, some decorated by such masters as Melozzo da Forlì, Giotto and Pollaiuolo, and the tombs of popes. The necropolis, even deeper underground, shelters pre-Christian tombs, as well as a simple monument which may have marked St. Peter's burial place. The excavated area is not open to general viewing and visits must be arranged in

Gilded magnificence for a papal mass in St. Peter's.

advance through the Vatican Tourist Office.

St. Peter's is open without interruption every day from 7 a.m. until sunset. Masses are said frequently in the side chapels, in various languages. Visitors wearing shorts, bare-backed dresses, miniskirts or other scanty attire are politely turned away.

Vatican Museums

The 7 kilometres (4 mi.) of rooms and galleries of the Vatican Museums offer a microcosm of Western civilization. It is all there in almost bewildering profusion, from Egyptian mummies, exquisite Etruscan gold jewellery and Greek and Roman sculpture, right through medieval and Renaissance masterpieces to modern religious art. On a single ticket you can visit eight museums, five galleries, the Apostolic Library, the Borgia Apartments and Raphael Rooms and, of course, the Sistine Chapel.

Once past the entrance doors, you ascend a wide spiral ramp, which somehow manages to suck in all the crowds and disperse them up through the galleries. There is a choice of tours, ranging from 1½ hours (A) to 5 hours (D). Here are some of the highlights:

With the booty from the ruthless dismantling of ancient monuments to make way for the Renaissance city in the 16th century, the **Pio-Clementino Museum** has assembled a wonderful collection of classical art. The most celebrated piece is the 1st-century B.C. *Laocoön* group of the Trojan priest and his sons strangled by serpents for offending Apollo. Famous in imperial times, it was unearthed from a vineyard on the Esquiline in 1506, to the delight of Michelangelo, who rushed to view it. It now stands in a recess of the charming octagonal Belvedere courtyard. Roman copies of other Greek sculptures, such as the *Aphrodite of Cnidos* of Praxiteles and the superb *Apollo*, achieved a fame as great as the originals, now lost. Take special note of the powerful muscular *Torso* by Apollonius which had such a profound influence on Renaissance artists and sculptors, in particular Michelangelo.

Some of archaeology's most exciting finds from a 7th-century B.C. Etruscan burial mound at Cerveteri (see p. 90) are displayed in the **Gregorian-Etruscan Museum**. The tomb yielded an abundance of treasures. Among the finely worked jewellery is an ornate gold brooch surprisingly decorated with lions and ducklings. Look out for the unusual bronze statue of a sprightly Etruscan warrior, the *Mars of Todi*, from the 4th century B.C.

Judging by the number of obelisks scattered throughout Rome, Egyptian art was much admired and sought after by the ancient Romans. The basis of the collection in the **Egyptian Museum** rests on finds from Rome and its surroundings,

particularly from the Gardens of Sallust between the Pincian and Quirinal hills, the Temple of Isis on the Campus Martius and Hadrian's Villa at Tivoli (see p. 86). The black granite throne of Rameses II is displayed, as well as a colossal statue of his mother, Queen Tuia.

Pope Julius II took a calculated risk in 1508 when he called in a relatively untried 25-year-old to decorate his new apartments. The result was the four **Raphael Rooms** *(Stanze di Raffaello)*. In the central Stanza della Segnatura are the two masterly frescoes, *Disputation over the Holy Sacrament*

Graceful ramp leads to laby-rinth of Vatican Museums.

and the *School of Athens*, confronting theological and philosophical wisdom. The *Disputation* unites biblical figures with historical pillars of the faith such as Pope Gregory and Thomas Aquinas, as well as painter Fra Angelico and the divine Dante. At the centre of the *School,* Raphael is believed to have given the red-robed Plato the features of Leonardo da Vinci, while portraying Michelangelo as the thoughtful Heraclitus, seated in the foreground.

For a stark contrast to Raphael's grand manner, seek out the gentle, luminous beauty of Fra Angelico's frescoes in the **Chapel of Nicholas V**. The lives of St. Lawrence and St. Stephen are depicted here in delicately subdued pinks and blues, highlighted with gold.

The lavishly decorated **Borgia Apartments** contain Pinturicchio's sublime frescoes, with portraits of lusty Pope Alexander VI and his notorious son Cesare and daughter Lucrezia, and lead into the modern religious art collection of Paul VI. This includes Rodin bronzes, Picasso ceramics, Matisse's Madonna sketches and designs for ecclesiastical robes and, somewhat unexpectedly, a grotesque Francis Bacon pope.

Rare literary treasures are on view in the Apostolic Library.

One of Europe's finest collections of rare books and ancient manuscripts is kept in the hallowed precincts of the **Apostolic Library**. In the great vaulted reading room, or Sistine Hall, designed by Domenico Fontana in 1588, ceilings and walls are covered in paintings of ancient libraries, conclaves, thinkers and writers. Showcases displaying precious illuminated manuscripts have replaced the old lecterns. A 1,600-year-old copy of Virgil's works, the poems of Petrarch, a 6th-century gospel of St. Matthew, and Henry VIII's love letters to Anne Boleyn are among the prize possessions.

Nothing can prepare you for the visual shock of the **Sistine Chapel** *(Capella Sistina)*, built for Sixtus IV in the 15th century. Even the discomfort of the throngs of visitors (silence requested) seems to yield to the power of Michelangelo's ceiling, his *Last Judgment* and the other wall frescoes by Botticelli, Pinturicchio, Perugino, Ghirlandaio, Rosselli and Signorelli. In this private chapel of popes, where the cardinals hold their conclave to elect a new pope, the glory of the Catholic Church achieves its finest artistic expression.

The chapel portrays nothing less than the biblical history of man, in three parts: from Adam to Noah; the giving of the Law to Moses; and from the birth of Jesus to the Last Judgment. Towards the centre of Michelangelo's **ceiling,** you'll make out the celebrated outstretched finger of the *Creation of Adam*. Most overwhelming of all is the impression of the whole—best appreciated looking back from the bench at the chapel's exit.

A controversial programme of restoration, which involves **71** cleaning the frescoes of the dust and grime of the centuries, has revealed an unsuspected brilliance of colour.

On the chapel's altar wall is Michelangelo's **Last Judgment**, begun 23 years after the ceiling, when he was 60 and imbued with deep religious soul-searching. An almost naked Jesus dispenses justice more like a stern, even fierce classical god-hero than the conventionally gentle biblical figure. The artist's agonizing self-portrait can be made out in the flayed skin of St. Bartholomew, to the right below Jesus.

Amid all the Vatican treasures, the 15 rooms of the **Picture Gallery** (*Pinacoteca Vaticana*) sometimes get short shrift. This collection of ten centuries of paintings began with 73 canvases returned from Paris (where Napoleon had taken them). A separate wing of the palace was built in 1922 by Milanese architect Luca Beltrami to house the expanded collection. Among the most important exhibits are works by Giotto, Fra Angelico, Perugino, Raphael's *Transfiguration* (his last great work), Leonardo da Vinci's unfinished *St. Jerome* in sombre tones of sepia, Melozzo da Forlì's ethereal *Musician Angels* frescoes, Bellini's *Pietà* from a large

Man at Work
As might be imagined, painting the Sistine ceiling wasn't easy. Michelangelo, sculptor in marble with only a little oil painting behind him, had never before done a fresco (wall-painting on damp plaster). Preferring his inexperience to their incompetence, he fired his seven assistants in the first couple of weeks and continued alone for four years, from 1508 to 1512. He worked on tiptoe, bent backwards (he said) "like a Syrian bow"—not, as has been suggested, lying on his back. Pope Julius II kept a close eye on progress, climbing the scaffolding himself and threatening to throw Michelangelo off his platform if he didn't hurry up.

"I'm not in a good place," wrote Michelangelo to a friend, "and I'm no painter."

altarpiece, and Caravaggio's dramatic *Descent from the Cross*.

As you wander the galleries, glance out of the windows from time to time to view St. Peter's dome over the clipped hedges of the Vatican gardens (best views from the Gallery of the Maps). Take a rest in the **Cortile della Pigna,** dominated by the enormous bronze pinecone fountain (1st century A.D.) which gives the courtyard its name. And stop for a snack or refreshment at the self-service cafeteria.

The Janiculum
(Gianicolo)
After absorbing the riches of the Vatican, you can be forgiven for suffering a severe case of cultural overload. Rising above the Vatican, the Janiculum Hill provides the prescribed respite in the welcome shade of its parks. From the crest, you have a breathtaking view of Rome from the **Piazzale Garibaldi**. In the centre of the square stands an imposing bronze equestrian statue of the hero of the Risorgimento, who fought one of his fiercest battles here in 1849. From the crest, the road winds down into Trastevere (see p. 46).

The Sistine Chapel's frescoes have undergone a clean-up.

The Churches

You can't see them all. Don't try. There's one for every day of the year! On the other hand, what a pity to leave Rome without visiting at least some, for quite apart from their religious significance, many contain magnificent works of art.

Catholic pilgrims aim to visit all four great patriarchal basilicas: St. Peter's (see p. 64), Santa Maria Maggiore, St. John Lateran and St. Paul's Outside the Walls. And these top the list for most visitors. But numerous other churches can claim your attention for their architectural or artistic splendours or their historic interiors. We touch on only a representative selection of the best.

Santa Maria Maggiore

This largest and most splendid of all the churches dedicated to the Virgin Mary was first built in the 4th century by Pope Liberius over the site of a Roman temple to the goddess Juno on the Esquiline Hill. A century later it was torn down and rebuilt by Sixtus III.

Glittering **mosaics** enhance the perfect proportions of the interior. Above the 40 ancient Ionic columns of the triple nave, a mosaic frieze portrays Old Testament scenes leading up to the coming of Christ. The theme continues in the gilded Byzantine-style mosaics on the triumphal arch, detailing the birth and childhood of Jesus, and culminates in the magnificent 13th-century portrayal of Mary and Jesus enthroned, in the apse behind the high altar.

Inlaid red and green precious marbles pattern the floor in the cosmatesque style, first pioneered by Rome's Cosmati family of craftsmen in the 12th century. Note the opulence of the coffered Renaissance ceiling, gilded with the first shipment of gold from the Americas.

A casket of gold, silver and crystal below the high altar contains fragments reputed to come from the **holy crib**, brought back from the Holy Land by St. Helena, Constantine's mother.

The incomparably rich **Pauline Chapel** (Capella Paolina) has an altar inlaid with lapis lazuli, amethyst and agate below a revered 9th-century painting of the Madonna and Child. Every August 5th, white flower petals are showered onto the altar to mark the date when a miraculous fall of snow, prophesied by the Virgin, showed Pope Liberius where to build her church.

St. John Lateran
(San Giovanni in Laterano)

Regarded as the mother church of the Catholic world (it's the seat of the pope as Bishop of Rome), the original Lateran church predated even St. Peter's by a few years; Constantine built both basilicas in the early 4th century. Popes lived in the Lateran Palace for a thousand years until they moved to Avignon and then to the Vatican in the 14th century. On a wooden table, incorporated in the high altar, St. Peter himself is believed to have celebrated mass.

Fire, earthquake and looting by the Vandals reduced the church to ruins over the centuries. The present basilica, little more than 300 years old, is at least the fifth on this site. But the bronze central doors go all the way back to ancient Rome when they graced the entrance to the Curia in the Forum (see p. 49). High above the basilica's façade, 15 giant white statues of Jesus, John the Baptist and the sages of the Church stand out against the sky.

Transformed by Borromini in the 17th century, the interior gives a predominant impression of sombre white and grey, more restrained than is usual for Baroque architects, and enlivened only by the coloured marble inlays of the paving. In recesses along the nave stand majestic statues of the Apostles sculpted by pupils of Bernini.

The octagonal **baptistery** preserves some truly splendid 5th- and 7th-century mosaics. It was built over the baths of Constantine's second wife Fausta, where Rome's first baptisms took place. The beautiful bronze doors of St. John the Baptist's Chapel, removed from the Baths of Caracalla, sing musically on their hinges when opened.

Foremost exponents of the cosmatesque style of inlaid marble, brothers Jacopo and Pietro Vassalletto have excelled themselves in the **cloisters**, where alternating straight and twisted columns, set mosaic-style with coloured stone, create a perfect setting for meditation.

An ancient edifice opposite the basilica—almost all that's left of the old Lateran Palace—shelters the **Scala Santa**, the holy stairway brought back by St. Helena from Jerusalem and said to have been trodden by Jesus in the house of Pontius Pilate. The devout climb the 28 marble steps on their knees.

Outside the basilica stands an Egyptian **obelisk** brought from the Temple of Ammon in Thebes. It's the tallest in the world—31 metres (102 ft.)—

and the oldest (1449 B.C.) of the 13 still standing in Rome.

St. Paul's
Outside the Walls
(San Paolo fuori le Mura)

The basilica, largest in Rome after St. Peter's, was built by Constantine in 314 and later enlarged by Valentinian II and Theodosius. It survived astonishingly until destroyed by a tragic fire in 1823, but has been faithfully restored to its original splendour.

A tabernacle designed by the 13th-century sculptor Arnolfo di Cambio and retrieved from the ashes of the great fire decorates the high altar under which lies the burial place of St. Paul. After Paul was beheaded, a Roman matron, Lucina, placed the body here in her family vault. Constantine later encased it in a sarcophagus of marble and bronze, looted by Saracen invaders in 846.

Above the 86 Venetian marble columns runs a row of mosaic medallions representing all the popes from St. Peter to the present.

Pause in the peaceful Benedictine **cloisters**, designed by Pietro Vassalletto and surpassing even his work at St. John Lateran. Slender spiralled columns in the cosmatesque tradition glitter with green, red and gold mosaic, enclosing a garden of roses and gently rippling fountain.

San Clemente

This gem of a church hides a fascinating history which can be traced down through each of its three levels. The present **church,** dating back to the 12th

San Pietro in Vincoli harbours Michelangelo's majestic Moses.

century, is built in basilica form with three naves divided by antique columns and embellished by a pavement of cosmatesque geometric designs. A richly symbolic mosaic in the apse features the Cross as the Tree of Life nourishing all living things—birds, animals and plants.

To the right of the nave a staircase leads down to the 4th-century **basilica,** which underpins the present church. Sadly, the Romanesque frescoes—

copies show they were in near-perfect condition when uncovered earlier this century—have now drastically faded.

An ancient stairway leads further underground to a maze of corridors and chambers, believed to be the 1st-century home of St. Clement himself, third successor to St. Peter as pope. Down here is also the

The cloister at St. Paul's offers an oasis of peace.

earliest religious structure on this site, a pagan **temple** *(Mithraeum)* dedicated to the Eastern cult of the god Mithras. A well-preserved sculpture shows Mithras slaying a bull. The sound of trickling water from nearby streams echoes eerily through these subterranean chambers as it drains off into the Cloaca Maxima.

Santa Prassede

Though unremarkable from the outside, this little church is enchanting in the intimacy of its interior. St. Praxedes and her sister Pudentiana (her church is nearby) were the daughters of a Roman senator, who as one of the first converts to Christianity gave shelter to St. Peter.

Delicate 9th-century mosaics glittering with gold cover the walls and ceiling of the **Chapel of St. Zeno**, making it the city's most important Byzantine monument. It was designed as a tomb for Theodora, mother of Pope Paschal I. Medieval Romans called it the "Garden of Paradise" because of its beauty.

San Pietro in Vincoli

The church of St. Peter in Chains might not attract a second look (and might even prefer it that way, given the hordes of visitors), if it did not contain one of the greatest of Michelangelo's sculptures, his formidable **Moses**. Intended for St. Peter's Basilica as part of Michelangelo's botched project for Julius II's tomb, the statue of the great biblical figure sits in awesome majesty at the centre of the monument. The horns on his head continue a medieval mistranslation of the Hebrew word for halo-like rays of light. On each side, the comparatively passive figures of Jacob's wives—a prayerful Rachel and melancholy Leah—were Michelangelo's last completed sculptures.

The Empress Eudoxia founded the church in the 5th century, on the site of the Roman law court where St. Peter was tried and sentenced. It was built as a sanctuary for the chains with which Herod bound St. Peter in Palestine, together with those used when he was imprisoned in Rome. They are kept in a bronze reliquary under the high altar.

The Gesù

Severe and relatively discreet on its own piazza west of the Piazza Venezia, the Gesù is the mother church of the Jesuits and was a major element in their Counter-Reformation campaign. Begun as their Roman "headquarters" in 1568, its open ground plan was the model for the congregational churches that were to regain popular support from the Protestants. While its façade is more sober than the exultant Baroque churches put up as the movement gained momentum, the interior glorifies the new militancy in gleaming bronze, gold, marble and precious stones.

St. Ignatius Loyola, the Spanish soldier who founded the order, has a fittingly magnificent **tomb** under a richly decorated, almost overwhelming altar in the left transept, with a profusion of lapis lazuli. The globe at the top is said to be the largest piece of this stone in the world.

Sant'Ignazio

In gentler contrast, the church of Sant'Ignazio stands in an enchanting stage-set of russet and ochre Rococo houses. Inside, Andrea Pozzo (himself a Jesuit priest and designer of the saint's tomb in the Gesù) has painted a superb *trompe-l'œil* **ceiling fresco** (1685) depicting St. Ignatius' entry into paradise. Stand on a buff stone disk in the nave's central aisle and you will have the extraordinary impression of the whole building rising hundreds of feet above you through the ingenious architectural effect of the painting. From any other point, the columns appear to collapse. From another disk further up the aisle you can admire the celestial **dome** above the high altar, but as you advance, it begins to take on strange proportions: it is just another illusionist painting.

Museums

You could spend your entire visit to Rome just in museums. The city has yielded so much over the centuries that there is barely enough room to put it all on display. And invariably the collections are enhanced by the incomparable setting of an old palazzo or villa or ancient Roman building. Here are just a few among the very best (the Vatican Museums are described on p. 68, the Capitoline Museums on p. 28):

Borghese Gallery
(Galleria Borghese)
The avid and ruthless art patron Cardinal Scipione Borghese conceived this handsome Baroque villa in the Villa Borghese park as a home for his small but outstanding collection, using his prestige as nephew of Pope Paul V to ex-

tort coveted masterpieces from their owners.

The ground floor is devoted to **sculpture**, with works from antiquity, as well as by the young Bernini, in splendidly decorated rooms of marble and frescoes. As the cardinal's protégé, Bernini contributed busts of his patron, a vigorous *David* (said to be a youthful self-portrait), and a graceful sculpture of *Apollo and Daphne*, with the water-nymph turning into a laurel just as the god is about to seize her. In a later addition and star attraction, Canova portrays Napoleon's sister Pauline, who married into the Borghese family, as a naked reclining Venus.

On the first floor, the **picture gallery** boasts some exceptional paintings, with Raphael's *Descent from the Cross*, Titian's *Sacred and Profane Love*, Caravaggio's *David with the Head of Goliath* and *Madonna of the Serpent,* along with works by Rubens, Correggio, Veronese and Botticelli.

Villa Giulia

This pleasure palace of a pope, north-west of the Villa Borghese, is now the lovely setting for Italy's finest museum of **Etruscan art.** Although much about this pre-Roman civilization is still a mystery, the Etrus-cans left a wealth of detail about their customs and everyday life by burying the personal possessions of the dead with them in their tombs.

Replicas show the round stone burial mounds, built like huts. Room after room is filled with objects from the tombs—bronze statuettes of warriors in full battle dress; shields, weapons and chariots (even the skeletons of two horses); gold, silver and ivory jewellery; a large variety of decorative vases mass-imported by the Etrus-cans from Greece; and a host of everyday cooking utensils, mirrors and combs. Note the large bronze toilet box adorned with figurines of the Argonauts. The highlight is a life-size terracotta sculpture for a sarcophagus lid of a blissful young couple re-clining on a banquet couch.

Museo Nazionale Romano

You'll find your best introduction to the city's Greek and Roman antiquities in this superb collection housed in the Roman Baths of Diocletian.

Larger even than those of Caracalla, Diocletian's baths covered some 120 hectares (300 acres), part of which is now occupied by the Piazza della Repubblica and Michelangelo's church of Santa Maria degli Angeli, near Termini station.

The small cloister *(Piccolo Chiostro)* of the old Carthusian monastery, adapted from part of the baths, provides an attractive setting for the magnificent **Ludovisi Collection**, assembled by Cardinal Ludovico Ludovisi in the 17th century. Among the most important pieces, look for the marble altar-top known as the *Ludovisi Throne,* an orig-inal Greek work of the 5th century B.C., with exquisitely carved reliefs of Aphrodite and a maiden playing the flute; and the tragic statue of a barbarian warrior in the act of killing himself and his wife rather than submit to slavery.

In the so-called **"New Rooms"**, you'll find the *Apollo of the Tiber*, a copy of a bronze group by the young Phidias discovered in 1891 during excavations near the Palatine Bridge; a copy, probably the

The Borghese is the perfect home for these sublime sculptures.

best ever made, of Myron's famed *Discobolos* (Discus-Thrower); the *Daughter of Niobe*, a Greek original of the 5th century B.C.; the *Venus of Cyrene*; a bronze of a young man leaning on a lance; another of a seated boxer signed by Apollonius; and a variety of portrait sculptures, including one of Augustus. On the first floor, the **landscape frescoes** from the imperial villa of Livia show nature at its most bountiful, with flowers, trees, birds and luscious fruits painted with realistic attention to detail.

Galleria Nazionale d'Arte Antica

The Palazzo Barberini (Via delle Quattro Fontane) provided another architectural battleground for arch-rivals Borromini and Bernini, each of whom built one of its grand staircases and contributed to the superb façade. It is worth a visit as much for its Baroque décor as for its collection of paintings. Art and architecture converge in the palace's **Great Hall** with Pietro da Cortona's dazzling illusionist ceiling fresco, *Triumph of Divine Providence*.

The major part of the national art collection is hung in the first-floor gallery (the rest is housed in the Palazzo Corsini across the Tiber in Trastevere). Works include a Fra Angelico triptych, the celebrated portrait of *Henry VIII* by Hans Holbein, and paintings by Titian, Tintoretto, Perugino, Lorenzo Lotto and El Greco. Look out especially for Raphael's *La Fornarina*, the most famous of the many he painted of the baker's daughter who was his mistress.

Galleria Doria Pamphili

The vast Palazzo Doria in the Corso is still the private residence of the Doria family, but the public are allowed in several days a week to view their richly endowed private collection of paintings, assembled over hundreds of years.

Here's a case where you can't do without a catalogue, as the paintings are identifiable only by number. They hang three deep on either side of four galleries enclosing a Renaissance courtyard.

In this stunning collection, virtually every one of the paintings, mostly from the 15th to the 17th centuries, is a masterpiece. It covers works by Titian, Raphael, Veronese, Caravaggio, as well as painters of the Dutch and Flemish schools —Rembrandt and Van Dyck. Look out for the serene and evocative landscape of the

Flight into Egypt by Annibale Carracci, and the windswept *Naval Battle in the Bay of Naples* by Breughel the Elder.

You'll find a nice stylistic contrast in a little room off the galleries, which juxtaposes a brilliant worldly portrait by Velàzquez of Innocent X, the family pope elected in 1644, alongside a more serene marble bust of him by Bernini.

Excursions

The main excursions into the Lazio (Latium) countryside around Rome today are still those that ancient Romans took to vacation homes by the sea or nearby hills and lakes. But first you should take an important short trip just outside the city walls to the Old Appian Way.

▶ Old Appian Way
(Via Appia Antica)
As you head south-east through the Porta San Sebastiano, look back for a good view of the old **Aurelian Wall**, which still encloses part of Rome. Its massive defensive ramparts stretch into the distance, topped by towers and bastions built to resist the onslaught of barbarian invasions in the 3rd century.

Ahead lies a narrow lane, hemmed in at first by hedges

The Third City
The historic centre of Rome has been kept mercifully free of antagonistic 20th-century innovations. But there is an ultra-modern "Third Rome", 5 kilometres (3 mi.) south along the Ostian Way—Mussolini's dream, intended to rival the glories of the Imperial and Renaissance cities.

Known simply by its initials EUR (pronounced Ay-oor), this complex of massive white marble buildings, with wide avenues and green open spaces grouped around an artificial lake, was designed for a world fair in 1942 to mark 20 years of fascism. The war interrupted construction and the fair never took place.

In recent years, EUR has developed into a thriving township of government ministries, offices, conference centres and fashionable apartments. Several buildings remain from Mussolini's time, including the formidable cube of arches of the Palace of Workers *(Palazzo della Civiltà del Lavoro)*, known as the "Square Colosseum". For the 1960 Olympics, engineer Pier Luigi Nervi designed the huge domed Palazzo dello Sport. The Museum of Roman Civilization *(Museo della Civiltà Romana)* contains a fascinating model of ancient Rome.

and the high walls of film stars' and millionaires' homes— the **Old Appian Way**. When Appius Claudius the Censor opened it and gave it his name in 312 B.C., this was the grandest road the western world had ever known. You can still see some of the original basalt paving stones, over which the Roman legions marched on their way to Brindisi to set sail for the Levant and North Africa.

Since by law no burial could take place within the city walls, the tombs of the dead were built along this road. On either side lie the ruins of sepulchres of 20 generations of patrician families, some marked by simple tablets, others by impressive mausoleums. For the same reason, the Christians built their cemeteries in the catacombs here.

At a fork in the road, the chapel of **Domine Quo Vadis** marks the spot where St. Peter, fleeing from Nero's persecution in Rome, is said to have encountered Christ. "Whither goest thou, Lord?" asked Peter. ("Domine quo vadis?"). Christ replied: "I go to Rome to be crucified again." Ashamed of his fear, Peter turned back to Rome and his own crucifixion. The little chapel contains a copy of a stone with a footprint said to have been left by Christ (the original is in the Basilica of San Sebastiano).

Further along the Appia Antica, within a short distance of each other, are three of Rome's most celebrated catacombs, St. Calixtus, St. Sebastian and Domitilla. About 6 million early Christians, many of them martyrs and saints, were buried in some 50 of these vast underground cemeteries. Knowledgeable guides accompany you in groups into the labyrinth of damp and musty-smelling tunnels and chambers burrowed into the soft volcanic tufa rock, sometimes six levels deep (claustrophobes abstain). Paintings and carvings adorn the catacombs with precious examples of early Christian art.

The entrance to the **Catacombs of St. Calixtus** lies at the end of an avenue of cypresses. An official tour takes you down to the second level of excavations, where you will see the burial niches, called *loculi*, cut into the rock one above the other on either side of the dark galleries. Occasionally the narrow passageways open out into larger chambers or *cubicula*, where a whole family would be buried together. One such crypt sheltered the remains of 3rd-century popes; another held the body of St. Cecilia until it was transferred to the church of Santa Cecilia in Trastevere (the statue of the saint lying in a recess is a copy of the one by Stefano Maderno in the church, see p. 48).

In the **Catacombs of St. Sebastian**, the bodies of the Apostles Peter and Paul are said to have been hidden for several years during 3rd-century persecutions. You can still see graffiti in Latin and Greek invoking the two saints.

The cylindrical **tomb of Cecilia Metella** dominates the Appian landscape. This little-known noblewoman was a relative of the immensely rich Crassus who financed Julius Caesar's early campaigns. A Roman family of the 14th century added the castellated parapet when they turned it into a fortress.

Alongside extends the well-preserved **Circus of Maxentius** built for chariot races in A.D. 309 under the last pagan emperor, who carried out the final wave of Christian persecutions in Rome.

Turn off the Via Appia to visit the **Fosse Ardeatine**, a modern place of pilgrimage for Italians. In March 1944, in retaliation for the killing of 32 German soldiers by the Italian Resistance, the Nazis rounded

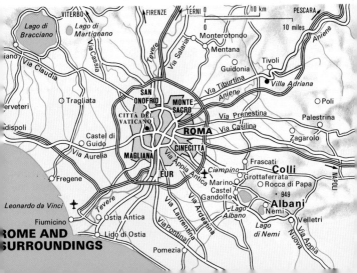

ROME AND
SURROUNDINGS

up at random 335 Italian men (10 for each killed and an extra 15 for good measure) and machine-gunned them down in the sandpits of the Via Ardeatina. As soon as the Germans left Rome, a poignant memorial was raised here to the dead, among them a boy of 14.

Tivoli

The picturesque town of Tivoli perches on a steep slope amid the woods, streams and twisted silvery olive trees of the Sabine Hills. Inhabited even in ancient times, when it was known as Tibur, Tivoli continued to prosper throughout the Middle Ages and thus preserves interesting Roman remains and medieval churches, as well as the famous Renaissance villa and gardens.

Public buses leave Rome regularly from Via Gaeta, opposite the Stazione Termini; the drive, 30 kilometres (19 mi.) along the old Roman chariot road (repaved) of the Via Tiburtina, takes about an hour and a quarter.

The **Villa d'Este**, sprawls along the hillside. From its windows and balconies, you look down on the **gardens**, falling away in a series of steep terraces—a paradise of dark cypresses, fountains (a reputed 500), grottoes, pools and statues.

Cardinal Ippolito II d'Este conceived this pleasure garden in the 16th century. Architect Pirro Ligorio, with that genius for playing with water that has characterized the Romans since ancient times, created it. On the Terrace of 100 Fountains jets of water splash into a long basin guarded by eagle statues. The grand Organ Fountain, originally accompanied by organ music, cascades steeply down the rocks. You can walk up behind it to view the gardens through a haze of spray. On the lowest level, three large deep pools contrast in their stillness with the rush and roar of the water elsewhere.

The architect took particular delight in strange fantasies, such as the row of sphinxes spurting water from their nipples, or hidden joke jets which sprayed the unsuspecting passer-by. Don't worry, you won't be in for any unpleasant shocks; the "water tricks" are no more.

Tucked away at the foot of the hills lie the haunting ruins of **Hadrian's Villa** *(Villa Adriana)*. Spread across 70 hectares (173 acres), this retirement hideaway of the great emperor-builder (the Pantheon in Rome, Hadrian's Wall across Britain) was designed to recapture some of the architectural marvels of his empire, especially the Greece he loved above all else—a travel memoir for his old age, filled with treasures that have since found their way to museums around the world.

Those arriving at the villa by public bus are dropped off at the main gate and ticket office. Tourist coaches and private cars continue up the drive to the car park within the grounds. An excellent scale model here will give you an overview of the whole. As you will see, this was more a miniature city than a villa, even if it was an emperor's. The monumental baths, separate Greek and Latin libraries, Greek theatre, temples and pavilions together make up the home of a man who drew no distinction between the pleasures of mind and body.

You enter the ruins through the colonnades of the Greek-style **Stoa Poikile** (Painted Portico), which leads to the main imperial residence. Adjoining the palace are guest rooms, their black and white mosaic floors still visible, and an underground passageway for the servants to move about unseen.

A curtain of water screens the view at Tivoli's Villa D'Este.

The enchanting **Villa dell'-Isola,** a pavilion surrounded by a little reflecting pool and circular portico, epitomizes all the magic of the place.

To the south, remnants of arches and copies of Greek-style caryatids (female statues used as pillars) surround the **Pool of Canopus** leading to the sanctuary of the Egyptian god Serapis.

Barbarians and museum collectors have removed most of the villa's treasures, but a stroll among the remaining pillars, arches and mosaic fragments in gardens running wild among the olive trees, cypresses and umbrella pines can be marvellously evocative of a lost world.

Ostia Antica

Excavations continue to uncover fascinating sections of what was once the seaport and naval base of ancient Rome. The long-buried city of Ostia stands at the mouth *(ostium)* of the Tiber, 23 kilometres (14 mi.) south-west of the capital on the shores of the Tyrrhenian Sea.

Sea-going vessels were unable to travel inland along the shallow Tiber, so river barges plied back and forth from the port, carrying Rome's food and building materials. In its palmiest days, Ostia had

Strawberries for lunch and a wide panorama, away from Rome's heat in the Alban Hills.

100,000 residents and boasted splendid baths, temples, a theatre and imposing houses.

Ostia's well-preserved ruins, set among cypress and pine, reveal more about the daily life and building methods of the ancient Romans than do those

of the capital. Excavations since the 19th century have unearthed warehouses, offices, apartment blocks known as *insulae* (islands) and private houses with gardens, built facing the sea and decorated with mosaics and murals.

The porticoed **Piazzale delle Corporazioni** (Corporations' Square) held 70 commercial offices round a central temple to Ceres, goddess of agriculture. Mottoes and emblems in mosaic in the pavement tell of the grain factors, caulkers, ropemakers and shipowners from many parts of the world who traded here.

The neighbouring **theatre** from the time of Augustus now hosts performances of classical plays translated into Italian. It is worth climbing the tiered seats for a view over the whole ruined city.

As in Rome, the **Forum** was the focus of city life, dominated at one end by the Capitol, a temple dedicated to Jupiter, **89**

Juno and Minerva and at the other end by the Temple of Rome and Augustus, with the Curia, seat of the municipal authorities, and the basilica or law courts lying between.

To see a typical private dwelling, visit the **House of Cupid and Psyche**, with rooms paved in marble built round a central garden courtyard. Nearby, a small **museum** traces the history of Ostia with statues, busts and frescoes excavated in the region.

The modern seaside resort of Ostia attracts crowds of weekend Romans, who flock to the beaches of grey sand. Swimming is not recommended on account of the pollution. Dine instead in one of the cheerful open-air restaurants.

Rome's metro runs to Ostia, as well as city buses and guided excursions. The trip takes about 45 minutes.

The Alban Hills and Castel Gandolfo

Immediately south-east of Rome, the scattered hill villages known locally as the *Castelli Romani* (Roman Castles) began as fortified refuges during the medieval civil wars. Today it's just the summer heat that drives the Romans out on daytrips to the vineyards of the Alban hills and lakes.

The pope has his summer home at **Castel Gandolfo**, above Lake Albano, where he relaxes in the huge late-Renaissance palace designed by Carlo Maderno, set in beautiful landscaped gardens. He holds audience on Wednesdays from mid-July to early September and blesses the thousands of pilgrims on Sunday at noon. The palace, gardens and Vatican Observatory in the grounds are closed to visitors.

A terrace near the papal palace looks down on the dark blue waters of **Lake Albano**, lying in an old forested volcanic crater hundreds of feet below.

The villages of Frascati, Grottaferrata, Marino and Rocca di Papa make delightful stops, not least of all for a cool glass of their estimable white wine, especially during the autumn grape-harvest festivals. In the mellow microclimate of **Lake Nemi**, strawberries are grown all year round, served—with cream or lemon juice—in Nemi's village park.

Cerveteri

If the Villa Giulia in Rome (see p. 80) and the Gregorian-Etruscan Museum in the Vatican (see p. 68) have whetted your curiosity about the Etruscans, it is worth making a trip to the ancient necropolis at Cerveteri,

43 kilometres (27 mi.) northwest of Rome.

Known in ancient times as Caere, it was one of the original 12 towns of the powerful Etruscan League (at one time Etruscan kings even ruled Rome). But the city declined in the 3rd century B.C., after it became a Roman dependency.

The scores of **tombs** discovered represent every kind of burial from the early shaft and pit graves to tumuli, dating from the 7th–1st centuries B.C. These later mounds often contain several chambers, carved into the volcanic tufa in the shape of wooden Etruscan homes. Stucco decorations and rock carvings represent the weapons, hunting equipment, domestic animals and even household pots and pans that the Etruscans felt they would still need in the after-life. Most famous is the Regolini-Galassi tomb, whose riches are now on display in the Vatican's Gregorian-Etruscan Museum.

Unfortunately many tombs have been plundered—and are still being plundered—by graverobbers. But the **Museo Nazionale di Cerveteri** in a 16th-century castle displays in chronological order a rich array of objects from the tombs, including sarcophagi, sculptures, wall-paintings and vases.

What to Do

Entertainment

Like every big city, Rome has its share of nightclubs and discotheques, but the most popular custom is to linger well past midnight over dinner in one of the attractive outdoor restaurants, serenaded by minstrels and guitarists (see p. 96).

Music. Almost every evening in July and August, there's outdoor opera (with *Aïda* a long-standing favourite) in the spectacular setting of the ruined Baths of Caracalla (see p. 58). The official opera season runs from November to June at the Teatro dell'Opera.

Summer concerts of classical music take place in picturesque and historic settings, such as the Campidoglio, Santa Maria Sopra Minerva and the Villa Medici.

Open-air festivals of jazz, pop and rock are held in the parks and gardens of Rome for the *Estate Romana* (Roman Summer).

Theatre. Several theatres stage classical and modern plays and musical comedies, almost always in Italian. Italian translations of classical plays are performed in the ancient **91**

Calendar of Events

January 5–6	*Befana* (Epiphany) Festival on Piazza Navona.
March 9	*Festa di Santa Francesca Romana*; Romans drive their cars to the Piazzale del Colosseo near the church of Santa Francesca Romana (also known as Santa Maria Nova) in the Forum, for blessing.
March–April	Good Friday; Pope leads the Procession of the Cross at 9 p.m. from the candlelit Colosseum to the Forum. Easter Sunday; Pope blesses the crowds from the balcony at St. Peter's at noon.
April	*Festa della Primavera* (Spring Festival); the Spanish Steps are decked with pink azaleas.
April 21	Anniversary of Rome's founding.
April/May	International Horse Show, with Nations' Cup, in Villa Borghese park.
May	Open-air art exhibition in Via Margutta. Antiques fair in Via dei Coronari. International tennis championship in Foro Italico.
June (first week)	*Festa della Repubblica*; military parade along Via dei Fori Imperiali.
June 29	*Festa di San Pietro e San Paolo*; solemn rites in St. Peter's and St. Paul's Outside the Walls.
July	*Noiantri* street festival in Trastevere.
August 5	*Festa della Madonna della Neve* in Santa Maria Maggiore.
August 15	*Ferragosto* or Feast of the Assumption; most Romans leave the city for the sea or hills.
September	Open-air art exhibition in Via Margutta.
December	Children's toy and Christmas decoration market on Piazza Navona.
December 8	*Festa della Madonna Immacolata* (Immaculate Conception); the pope or his envoys place flowers at the column of the Virgin in Piazza di Spagna.
December 24	Midnight mass at St. Peter's and at Santa Maria Maggiore with veneration of Holy Crib.
December 25	Nativity crib with revered Bambino in Santa Maria in Aracoeli.

theatre at the seaside resort of Ostia (see p. 88).

Cinema. Rome has about 100 cinemas, but few show films in their original language; foreign films are dubbed in Italian. The *Pasquino* in Trastevere offers the original sound track. Rome's cinemas are almost always filled to capacity.

Shopping

Rome's international reputation as a marvellous shopping city is unquestionably deserved. Nowhere is the Italian flair for display more striking than in the chic boutiques, and the shop assistants, even if they don't speak English, will bend over backwards to be helpful.

Where to Shop
Rome's most fashionable shopping district is found between the Spanish Steps and Via del Corso, notably along Via Condotti, Via Frattina and Via Borgognona. Some of Europe's finest shops and boutiques are here, but while bargains can occasionally be found, Roman shoppers who know go elsewhere—and pay considerably less.

A favoured shopping street is the Via Cola di Rienzo on the right bank of the Tiber. Prices are also reasonable around Via del Tritone, near the Trevi Fountain, and in the twisting streets near the Campo de' Fiori and the Pantheon.

For quality goods, Italians prefer shopping in small boutiques with a long tradition, very often a family business guaranteeing generations of craftsmanship. As a result, you won't find upmarket department stores, but popular, low-price chain stores, such as Rinascente or Upim.

Rome's incredible flea market, the Porta Portese, extends for about 4 kilometres (2½ mi.) of streets and alleys. It begins at a battered archway, the Porta Portese, just across the Tiber at the Ponte Sublicio. Invariably jammed, Porta Portese operates on Sundays from dawn to about 1 p.m. The cluttered stalls offer everything from refrigerators to kittens, with the emphasis on clothing. Look out especially for the Abruzzi peasant rugs and bedspreads. Traveller's cheques are accepted at many of the market stalls. But leave any unnecessary money or documents behind; pickpockets love this place. Other outdoor markets during the week are on Via Sannio and Piazza Vittorio Emanuele II. **93**

What to Buy

Antiques. If you are looking for genuine, authenticated antiques—silver, paintings, jewellery or furniture—stick to reputable dealers rather than the open-air markets. Quality shops will provide a certificate of guarantee *(certificato di garanzia)* and will arrange international shipping, while taking care of all the formalities. The best antique shops are to be found in the streets around the Piazza di Spagna (especially in Via del Babuino) and in the area west of the Corso Vittorio Emanuele, not to mention the Via dei Coronari (see p. 40).

Ceramics. Carafes, jugs, plates, bowls, etc., with attractive and colourful designs make decorative as well as useful gifts.

Fashion. From ultra-chic to sports clothes and ready-to-wear, Italian design is unsurpassed. Women's fashions include the major French designers, as well as the natives (such as Valentino, Armani, Gianni Versace and Missoni). The men's clothes meccas are Cucci (with a C) and Battistoni. Children's clothing is not neglected, and no less expensive either, with some superb items in Tablò's two shops.

Food and wine. Possibilities are inevitably limited because of the problems of transportation, but you can take home without too much risk a block of parmesan, which travels and keeps well, salamis, the Parma and San Daniele ham *(prosciutto crudo)*, and to accompany them, Rome's local vintages from the Alban Hills (see p. 90).

Jewellery. Italian gold- and silversmiths are among the best and most prolific in Europe. For sheer exclusivity, if you can afford the price, brave the

imposing marble façade of Bulgari on Via Condotti. Costume jewellery is also a good buy.

Leather. Especially shoes, but also gloves, bags, wallets, jackets, belts, desk sets and luggage are of impeccable quality and design. Some of the finest leather goods can be found at Gucci, Fendi or Pier Caranti.

Souvenirs. When it comes to mass-produced souvenirs, you will find endless invention in the realm of the cheap—and not so cheap—and nasty: Trevi Fountain water squirters, Colosseum with plaster Christians fed to plastic lions, glass balls of the pope blessing the faithful in a snow storm...

Textiles. You'll find a wide range of quality silks—blouses, shirts, suits, scarves and ties—and knitwear with colourful and distinctive patterns.

Window-shopping along the Corso is one of the joys of the evening stroll.

Eating Out

Do as the Romans do so enthusiastically and turn your eating out into an evening out. They like to spend hours over a leisurely meal of innumerable courses in the genial company of family or friends in one of the pleasant *trattorie* or restaurants which abound in the city. And with the banning of traffic in sections of Rome's historic centre, not to mention a benevolent climate, outdoor dining is once more a delight.

Choice spots are Trastevere (see p. 46), which boasts hundreds of little *trattorie*, and the Jewish Ghetto (see p. 43), with its own specialities. Still in the tracks of the Romans, drive out at least once into the countryside beyond the walls to lunch or dine in one of the restaurants along the Via Appia Antica or the roads to the Alban Hills or Ostia.

Where to Eat

Only in a few hotels catering to tourists will you find an English or American-style breakfast. Otherwise head for a good *caffè* on the piazza and settle happily for the *prima colazione* of superb coffee, espresso black or *cappuccino* with foaming hot milk (sprinkled in the best establishments with powdered chocolate), and toast or sweet roll. Italian tea is somewhat anemic, but the hot chocolate is excellent.

For those adopting a healthy "sightseer's diet" of one main meal a day, preferably in the evening, the ideal place for a lunch-time snack is a stand-up bar serving *tavola calda* ("hot table"). All through the day, without interruption, you can choose from a variety of hot and cold dishes—sandwiches, pasta, fish and chips, spit-roasted chicken, and slices of pizzas with different rich toppings—to take away or eat on the spot.

In theory, a *ristorante* is a fancier and larger establishment than a family-style *trattoria*. But in Rome the distinction is blurred beyond recognition; they're both ways of saying restaurant, as is the less frequent *osteria*. A *trattoria-pizzeria* will serve pizza in addition to the standard *trattoria* fare.

Price should not be taken as an indication of the quality of the cooking; an expensive restaurant may offer a superb meal with service to match, but you may also be paying for the location. Only a few steps away from such famous tourist spots as the Piazza del Popolo and the Piazza Navona, you'll find numerous little *trattorie*, with considerably lower prices, where the ambience, half the value of an Italian meal, is infinitely more enjoyable and the food has more real character. Don't expect to find too much character in the hotel dining room.

Many restaurants display the menu with prices in a glass case outside, so you will have an idea of what's on offer, without any obligation to go inside.

When to Eat

Roman restaurants serve lunch from 12.30 to 3 p.m. and dinner from 7.30 to midnight. Each is closed one day a week, which will vary from restaurant to restaurant. If you are set on a particular restaurant, it's wise to book a table by telephone, especially at peak hours (around 1.30 and 9 p.m.).

What to Eat

Any *trattoria* worth its olive oil will set out on a long table near the entrance a truly painterly display of its **antipasti** (hors d'oeuvre). The best way to get to know the delicacies is to make up your own assortment *(antipasto misto)*. Both attractive and tasty are the cold *peperoni*: red, yellow and green peppers grilled, skinned and marinated in olive oil and lemon juice. Mushrooms *(funghi)*, baby marrows *(zucchini)*, aubergines *(melanzane)*, artichokes *(carciofi)* and sliced fennel *(finocchio)* are also served cold, with a dressing *(pinzimonio)*. One of the most refreshing *antipasti* is the *mozzarella alla caprese*, slices of soft white buffalo cheese and tomato in a dressing of fresh basil and olive oil. Ham from Parma comes paper thin with melon *(prosciutto con melone)* or, better still, fresh figs.

Popular **soups** are mixed vegetable *(minestrone)* and clear soup *(brodo)*, with a beaten egg in it *(stracciatella)*.

Pasta is usually the first of at least three courses. While you are not strictly obliged to emulate the Italians, waiters will raise a sad eyebrow if you make a whole meal out of a plate of spaghetti. But foreigners will be foreigners.

It is said that there are as many forms of pasta as there are French cheeses—some 360 at last count, with new forms being created every year. Each sauce—tomato, cream, cheese, meat or fish—needs its own kind of noodle. As well as spaghetti and macaroni, other names will be familiar: baked *lasagne* with layers of pasta, meat sauce and béchamel, **97** rolled *cannelloni*, stuffed *ravioli*, and *fettucine* or *tagliatelle* ribbon noodles. From there you launch into the lusty poetry of *tortellini, cappelletti* and *agnolotti* (all variations of *ravioli*), or curved *linguine*, flat *pappardelle*, feather-like *penne*, corrugated *rigatoni* and potato or semolina *gnocchi*. Discover the other 346 for yourselves.

And there are almost as many sauces. The most famous is, of course, *bolognese*, also called *ragù*; the best includes not only minced beef, tomato puree and onions, but chopped chicken livers, ham, carrot, celery, white wine and nutmeg. Other popular sauces range from the simple (but flavourful) *pomodoro* (tomato, garlic and basil), *aglio e olio* (garlic, olive oil and chilli peppers), *carbonara* (diced bacon and egg), *matriciana* (salt pork and tomatoes), *pesto* (basil and garlic ground up in olive oil with pine nuts and pecorino cheese) to *vongole* (clams and tomatoes).

Another Italian invention familiar around the world, the **pizza** is a much more elaborate affair than you may be used to. Toppings may include the following ingredients: tomato, ham, cheese, mushrooms, peppers, anchovies, artichoke hearts, egg, clams, tuna fish, garlic—or any other ingredient that takes the cook's fancy. It is a popular midnight snack, especially after the opera or theatre.

The main course will be a hearty **meat** dish. Veal has pride of place, with Rome's great speciality *saltimbocca* (literally "jump in the mouth", a veal roll with ham, sage and Marsala wine. Try the pan-fried cutlet *(costoletta)* in breadcrumbs, or *scaloppine al limone* (veal fillets with lemon). *Osso buco* is veal shinbone cooked in butter, with tomatoes, onions and mushrooms.

Beef *(manzo)* and pork *(maiale)* are most often served plain, charcoal-grilled or roast *(arrosto* or *al forno)*. Grilled Florentine T-bone *(bistecca alla fiorentina)* is the emperor of steaks and costs a royal ransom, but you should splash out and try it once. After that, the lesser proportions of the *bistecca* or *filetto* are something of an anticlimax. Romans claim the best roast kid *(capretto)*, sucking pig *(porchetta)* —roasted whole on a spit or spring lamb *(abbacchio)*, flavoured with garlic, sage and rosemary, dusted with flour, and seasoned just before serving with anchovy paste. The most common chicken dishes are grilled *(pollo alla diavola)* or filleted with ham and cheese *(petti di pollo alla bolognese)*.

Fish is prepared simply—grilled, steamed or fried. You may find scampi, prawns *(gamberi)*, mussels *(cozze)*, fresh sardines *(sarde)*, but also chewily delicious squid *(calamari)* and octopus *(polpi)*. You should also look out for sea bass *(spigola)*, red mullet *(triglia)* and swordfish *(pesce spada)*. The *fritto misto di pesce* is mixed fried seafood, mostly shrimp and octopus.

Vegetable accompaniments must be ordered separately, as they do not automatically come with the meat dish. What is available will depend on the season, but you are most likely to find spinach *(spinaci)*, endives *(cicoria)*, green beans *(fagioli)* done in butter and garlic, peas *(piselli)* and baby marrow *(zucchini)*. Aristocrats among the vegetables are the big boletus mushrooms *(funghi porcini)*, which sometimes come stuffed *(ripieni)* with bacon, garlic, parsley and cheese. The white truffle is an autumn delicacy. Try red peppers stewed with tomatoes *(peperonata)* or

This waiter happily shows that pasta is a well-balanced diet.

aubergine stuffed with anchovies, olives and capers. The Jewish Ghetto originated the spectacular *carciofi alla giudea*, whole artichokes, crisply fried, stem, heart, leaves and all.

Of the **cheeses**, the famous parmesan *(parmigiano)*, far better than the exported product, is also eaten separately, not just grated over soup or pasta. The cheese board may also offer blue *gorgonzola*, *provolone* buffalo cheese, creamy *fontina*, the pungent cow's milk *taleggio* or ewe's milk *pecorino*. *Ricotta* can be sweetened with sugar and cinnamon.

Dessert means first and foremost *gelati*, the creamiest ice-cream in the world. But it's generally better in an ice-cream parlour *(gelateria)*, of which there is an abundance in Rome, than in the average *trattoria*. *Zuppa inglese* (literally "English soup"), the Italian version of trifle, can be anything from an extremely thick and sumptuous mixture of fruit, cream, cake and Marsala to a disappointing sickly slice of cake. You may prefer the coffee-flavoured trifle *(tirami sù)*. The *zabaglione* of whipped egg yolks, sugar and Marsala

Old-time surroundings and music add charm to an evening out.

should be served warm or sent back.

The fruits of the season *(frutta della stagione)* can be a succulent alternative: strawberries *(fragole)* or the tiny, sweet wild strawberries *(fragolini del bosco)*, served with whipped cream or lemon juice; grapes *(uva)*, apricots *(albicocche)*, and fresh figs *(fichi)*, both black and green.

Drinks

All restaurants, no matter how small, will offer the open wine of the house, red or white, in one-quarter, half-litre or litre carafes, as well as a good selection of bottled vintages.

Rome's "local" wine comes from the surrounding province of Lazio, where the rich volcanic soil gives a special aroma. The whites from the Alban Hills, called Castelli Romani, are light and pleasant and can be sweet or dry. The most famous is Frascati.

From further afield, the Chiantis of Tuscany and Umbria are available everywhere; as are the lovely velvety Valpolicella, Barolo and Gattinara. Falerno, a wine which was popular already in the time of the Caesars, is still a favourite today. Look out for the unusually named Est! Est! Est! from Montefiascone.

Italian beer is increasing in popularity; it is not as strong as north European brands. Italians will also order mineral water *(acqua minerale)* with their meal. You can ask for it fizzy *(gasata)* or still *(naturale)*.

Among aperitifs, bitters such as Campari and Punt e Mes are refreshing with soda and lemon. Many vermouths tend to be sweet rather than dry. For after-dinner drinks, try the anis-flavoured *sambuca* with a *mosca* ("fly") coffee bean swimming in it, or *grappa* eau-de-vie distilled from grapes.

Prices and Tips

While some restaurants offer fixed-price, three-course meals *(menu turistico* or *prezzo fisso)* which will save money, you'll almost always get better food by ordering dishes individually.

Warning: by law all restaurants must now issue a formal receipt indicating the value added tax (I.V.A.). A customer may be stopped outside the premises and fined if unable to produce a receipt to show the tax has been paid. The bill usually includes cover *(coperto)* and service *(servizio)*.

It's customary to leave the waiter about 5—10 per cent of the bill. Never tip the owner, no matter how much he fusses over you—he'd be offended. **101**

To Help You Order...

What do you recommend?
Do you have a set menu?

Cosa consiglia?
Avete un menù a prezzo fisso?

I'd like a/an/some...

Vorrei...

beer	**una birra**	napkin	**un tovagliolo**
bread	**del pane**	pepper	**del pepe**
butter	**del burro**	potatoes	**delle patate**
coffee	**un caffè**	salad	**dell'insalata**
cream	**della panna**	salt	**del sale**
fish	**del pesce**	soup	**una minestra**
fruit	**della frutta**	sugar	**dello zucchero**
ice-cream	**un gelato**	tea	**un tè**
meat	**della carne**	(iced) water	**dell'acqua (fredda)**
milk	**del latte**	wine	**del vino**

...and Read the Menu

aglio	garlic	**manzo**	beef
agnello	lamb	**mela**	apple
albicocche	apricots	**melanzana**	aubergine
aragosta	spiny lobster	**merluzzo**	cod
arancia	orange	**ostrica**	oyster
bistecca	beef steak	**pancetta**	bacon
braciola	chop	**peperoni**	peppers, pimentos
brodetto	fish soup		
bue	beef	**pesca**	peach
calamari	squid	**pesce**	fish
carciofi	artichokes	**piselli**	peas
cavolo	cabbage	**pollo**	chicken
cicoria	endive	**pomodoro**	tomato
cipolle	onions	**prosciutto**	ham
coniglio	rabbit	**rognoni**	kidneys
cozze	mussels	**salsa**	sauce
crostacei	shellfish	**sarde**	sardines
fagioli	beans	**sogliola**	sole
fegato	liver	**stufato**	stew
fichi	figs	**tonno**	tunny (tuna)
formaggio	cheese	**uova**	eggs
funghi	mushrooms	**uva**	grapes
gamberi	scampi, prawns	**vitello**	veal
102 lamponi	raspberries	**vongole**	clams

BLUEPRINT for a Perfect Trip

How to Get There

If the choice of ways to go is bewildering, the complexity of fares and regulations can be downright stupefying. A reliable travel agent will have full details of all the latest flight possibilities, fares and regulations.

BY AIR

Rome's Fiumicino (Leonardo da Vinci) airport is on intercontinental air routes and is linked by frequent services to cities in Europe, North America, the Middle East and Africa.

Flying times: New York–Rome 8 hours; Los Angeles–Rome 15 hours; London–Rome 2½ hours; Sydney–Rome 26 hours.

BY CAR

Cross-Channel car-ferries link the U.K. with France, Belgium and Holland. Once on the continent, you can put your car on a train to Milan (starting points include Boulogne, Paris, Cologne). Or you can drive from the Channel coast to Rome without ever leaving a motorway. The main north-south (Milan–Florence–Regio–Calabria) and east-west (L'Aquila–Civitavecchia) motorways connect with Rome via a huge ring motorway *(grande raccordo anulare)*.

BY RAIL

Inter-Rail and Rail Europ Senior cards are valid in Italy, as is the Eurailpass for non-European residents (sign up before you leave home). Within Italy, you can obtain an Italian Tourist Ticket *(Biglietto Turistico di Libera Circolazione)* for unlimited first- or second-class rail travel for 8, 15, 21, or 30 days. The Kilometric Ticket *(Biglietto Chilometrico)* can be used by up to 5 people, even if not related, and is good for 20 trips or 3,000 kilometres, first or second class, over two months.

When to Go

Rome can be a city of extremes. From mid-June to mid-September, temperatures range from hot to very hot. Winters are cool, even cold, and at times rainy, with occasional snow, but often with days of warm sunshine. Spring and autumn are pleasantly mild.

		J	F	M	A	M	J	J	A	S	O	N	D
Maximum	°F	52	55	59	66	74	82	87	86	79	71	61	55
	°C	11	13	15	19	23	28	30	30	26	22	16	13
Minimum	°F	40	42	45	50	56	63	67	67	62	55	49	44
	°C	5	5	7	10	13	17	20	20	17	13	9	6

*Minimum temperatures are measured just before sunrise, maximum temperatures in the afternoon.

Planning Your Budget

To give you an idea of what to expect, here's a list of average prices in lire (L.). However, remember that all prices must be regarded as *approximate*.

Airport transfer. Train Fiumicino airport–Piramide railway station L. 5,000, then metro to Termini central railway station L. 700. Bus from Ciampino airport to Anagnina metro station L. 700. Taxi from Fiumicino to city centre L. 50,000–60,000.

Baby-sitters. L. 10,000 per hour, plus transport plus L. 10,000 agency fee.

Buses (city) **and metro.** Standard fare L. 800, one-day ticket L. 2,800, 7 days L. 10,000.

Camping. L. 7,700 per person per night, caravan (trailer) or camper L. 7,000, tent L. 3,900, car L. 4,000, motorbike L. 1,600.

Car hire. *Fiat Panda 45* L. 150,000 per day with unlimited mileage, L. 735,000 per week with unlimited mileage. *Alfa 33* L. 260,000 per day with unlimited mileage, L. 1,150,000 per week with unlimited mileage.

Cigarettes (packet of 20). Italian brands L. 2,950 and up, imported brands L. 3,250.

Entertainment. Cinema L. 8,000, discotheque (entry and first drink) L. 20,000–30,000, outdoor opera L. 30,000–90,000.

Hairdressers. *Woman's* shampoo and set or blow-dry L. 30,000–50,000, permanent wave L. 100,000–120,000. *Man's* haircut L. 10,000–25,000, L. 20,000–40,000 with shampoo.

Hotels (double room with bath, including tax and service). ***** L. 440,000–500,000, **** L. 390,000–495,000, *** L. 300,000–350,000, ** L. 186,000–285,000, * L. 90,000–150,000.

Meals and drinks. Continental breakfast L. 5,000, lunch/dinner in fairly good establishment L. 30,000–40,000, coffee served at a table L. 3,000–5,000, served at the bar L. 900–1,500, bottle of beer L. 4,000–6,000, soft drinks L. 1,500–3,000, aperitif L. 5,000 and up.

Museums. L. 2,000–10,000.

Shopping bag. 500 g. of bread L. 1,200, 250 g. of butter L. 2,900 and up, 6 eggs L. 1,300 and up, 500 g. of beefsteak L. 11,000, 200 g. of coffee L. 3,000 and up, bottle of wine L. 3,000 and up.

Taxis. Minimum charge L. 6,500 for the first 9 minutes or 3 km, L. 300 for each successive 45 seconds or 240 metres. Surcharge for night-time, holiday, and each piece of luggage.

An A–Z Summary of Practical Information and Facts

> Listed after some entries is the appropriate Italian translation, usually in the singular, plus a number of phrases that may come in handy during your stay in Italy.

A **ACCOMMODATION** (see also CAMPING). Rome's array of lodgings ranges from small, family-style boarding-houses *(pensione)* to de-luxe hotels *(albergo* or *hotel)*. In summer, booking ahead is important, but for the rest of the year you can normally find accommodation in your preferred category without difficulty. The Italian Tourist Office has up-to-date hotel information at the air terminal in Termini railway station.

If you plan to walk to most of Rome's sights, as you should, choose a hotel in the *centro storico* (historic centre), rather than in the suburbs. The saving in transport costs should compensate for the slightly higher rates in the centre of town.

As much as 20% in taxes and service charges may be added to the hotel rates listed on p. 105.

On its periphery, Rome has several motels. Some Roman Catholic institutions also take guests at reasonable rates.

Youth hostels *(ostello della gioventù)* are open to holders of membership cards issued by the International Youth Hostels Federation, or by the A.I.G. *(Associazione Italiana Alberghi per la Gioventù),* the Italian Youth Hostels Association, at:

Via Carlo Poma, 2; tel. 38 59 43

Day hotels *(albergo diurno)*. Rome has several of these "day-time" hotels, one of them at Termini railway station. They provide bathrooms, hairdresser and left-luggage facilities.

I'd like a single/double room.	**Vorrei una camera singola/matrimoniale.**
with bath/shower	**con bagno/doccia**
What's the rate per night?	**Qual è il prezzo per notte?**

AIRPORTS *(aeroporto)*. Rome is served by two airports, **Leonardo da** **Vinci,** commonly referred to as Fiumicino, near the seaside, 30 km. (22 mi.) south-west of the city, and **Ciampino,** 16 km. (10 mi.) southeast on the Via Appia Nuova. Fiumicino handles mainly scheduled air traffic, while Ciampino is used by most charter companies. Fiumicino has two terminals, one for domestic and one for international flights, a five-minute walk apart.

Airport information: Fiumicino, tel. 601 21
                                          Ciampino, tel. 46 94 or 72 44 21

Ground transport. From Fiumicino, take a train to Piramide station, and from there catch the metro for Termini railway station in the centre of town. Buses leave Ciampino every 30 minutes for Anagnina, where you can pick up the metrò to Rome. City air terminal:

Via Giolitti, 36; tel. 46 46 13

Check-in time is one hour and a half before departure for international flights, 30 minutes before domestic flights. Luggage may be checked in only at the airport. A few hours before your flight is due to leave, have your hotel receptionist telephone both the airport and city air terminal to enquire about any delay.

Porter!	**Facchino!**
Take these bags to the	**Mi porti queste valige fino**
bus/taxi, please.	**all'autobus/al taxi, per favore.**

ANIMAL WELFARE. An animal welfare association will take care of any animals found cruelly treated or in distress:

World Society for the Protection of Animals, tel. 86 80 01 63

BABY-SITTERS. Hotels can usually arrange for a reliable baby-sitter. Italian newspapers carry baby-sitter advertisements under the heading "Bambinaia". Agencies are also listed in English in the telephone directory under "Baby Sitters"; you will probably need to phone a couple of days in advance.

Can you get me a baby-sitter	**Può trovarmi una bambinaia per**
for tonight?	**questa sera?**

BICYCLE AND MOTORSCOOTER HIRE. You can hire bicycles from several locations, including Piazza del Popolo. A telephone hire service offers delivery at your hotel. Scooter-hire shops can be found in Via

B Cavour and Via della Purificazione. To hire a scooter, you have to be over 21.

C **CAMPING.** Rome and the surrounding countryside have some 20 official campsites, mostly equipped with electricity, water and toilet facilities. They are listed in the yellow pages of the telephone directory under "Campeggio–Ostelli–Villaggi Turistici". You can also contact the tourist office (see TOURIST INFORMATION OFFICES) for a comprehensive list of sites and rates. The Touring Club Italiano (TCI) and the Automobile Club d'Italia (ACI) publish lists of campsites and tourist villages, available at bookstores or the tourist office.

It is inadvisable to camp outside official sites. If you must, at least choose sites where there are other campers and always obtain permission from the owner of the property or the local authorities.

If you enter Italy with a caravan (trailer), you must be able to show an inventory (with two copies) of the material and equipment in the caravan: dishes, linen, etc.

May we camp here?	**Possiamo campeggiare qui?**
Is there a campsite near here?	**C'è un campeggio qui vicino?**
We have a tent/caravan (trailer).	**Abbiamo la tenda/la roulotte.**

CAR HIRE (*autonoleggio*). Major international car rental firms are represented in Rome and have offices at the airports; they are listed in the yellow pages of the telephone directory. Your hotel receptionist may be able to recommend a less expensive local firm.

You will need a valid driving licence. Minimum age varies from 21 to 25 according to the company. A deposit is often required if you are not paying with a credit card. It is possible to rent a car in one Italian city and turn it in in another.

I'd like to rent a car (tomorrow).	**Vorrei noleggiare una macchina (per domani).**
for one day	**per un giorno**
for one week	**per una settimana**

CIGARETTES, CIGARS AND TOBACCO (*sigarette, sigari, tabacco*). Tobacco products are a state monopoly and price-controlled in Italy and can only be sold in official tobacconists—recognizable by a large sign with a white *T* on a dark background which is mounted over the entrance—or at authorized hotel newsstands and café counters. Foreign brands cost as much as 50% more than domestic makes.

Smoking is prohibited on public transport and in taxis, in most cinemas and theatres, and in some shops.

I'd like a packet of…	**Vorrei un pacchetto di…**
with/without filter	**con/senza filtro**
I'd like a box of matches.	**Per favore, mi dia una scatola di fiammiferi.**

COMMUNICATIONS (see also Hours)

Post offices (*posta* or *ufficio postale*) handle telegrams, mail and money transfers. Postage stamps are also sold at tobacconists and at some hotel desks. Post boxes are red. The slot marked *Per la città* is for local mail only; the one marked *Altre destinazioni* is for all other destinations. Post to and from Italy can be slow; the Vatican operates well for outgoing mail, but you must buy the Vatican stamps.

Poste Restante/General Delivery (*fermo posta*). For a short stay it is not worth arranging to receive mail. However, there is a poste restante service at the main post office in Piazza San Silvestro. Don't forget your passport for identification when you go to pick up mail. You will have to pay a small fee.

Telegrams (*telegramma*). These can be sent to destinations inside and outside Italy, as can telex messages. There is now a rapidly growing telefax (facsimile) service.

Telephone (*telefono*). Public telephone booths are scattered at strategic locations throughout the city, as well as in almost every bar and café, indicated by a yellow sign showing a telephone dial and receiver. Buy tokens from the cashier before making your call. The main public telephone office, in the Palazzo delle Poste in Piazza San Silvestro, is open from 8.30 a.m. to 7.45 p.m.

Older types of public payphones require tokens (*gettoni*) with a value of 200 lire (available at bars, hotels, post offices and tobacconists); modern ones, with two separate slots, take both *gettoni* and coins.

From telephones labelled *Teleselezione* you can make direct international calls, but be sure to have a good supply of coins or tokens. Some telephones will take phone cards to the value of 5,000 or 10,000 lire, available at SIP (Italian Telephone Service) offices.

The normal dialling tone is a series of long dash sounds. A dot-dot-dot series means the central computer is overloaded; hang up and try again.

English-speaking operators of the ACI's telephone assistance service provide tourists with information and advice of all kinds. Dial 116.

Some useful numbers:

Local directory and other Italian enquiries	12
European international operator	15
Intercontinental operator	170
International telegrams	185

Give me…gettoni, please.	**Per favore, mi dia…gettoni.**
Can you get me this number in…?	**Può passarmi questo numero a…?**
I'd like a stamp for this letter/postcard.	**Desidero un francobollo per questa lettera/cartolina.**

COMPLAINTS (*reclamo*). Observe the cardinal rule of commerce in Italy: come to an agreement in advance—the price, the supplements, the taxes and the services to be received, preferably in writing. In hotels, shops and restaurants, complaints should be made to the manager (*direttore*) or the proprietor (*proprietario*).

Any complaint about a taxi fare should be settled by referring to the notice, in four languages, affixed by law in each taxi, specifying charges in excess of the meter rate.

For theft and other serious complaints, contact the police (see POLICE).

CONSULATES and EMBASSIES (*consolato; ambasciata*). The telephone directory lists all diplomatic representatives. The main ones for English-speaking visitors are:

Australia	Via Alessandria, 215; tel. 83 27 21
Canada	Via G. Battista de Rossi, 27; tel. 841 5341/4
Eire	Largo del Nazareno, 3; tel. 678 25 41
South Africa	Via Tanaro, 14–16; tel. 841 9794
United Kingdom	Via XX Settembre, 80; tel. 482 54 41
U.S.A.	Via Vittorio Veneto, 119; tel. 46 741

CONVERSION CHARTS. Italy uses the metric system. For fluid and distance measures, see p. 114–115.

Temperature

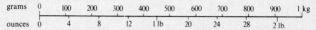

Weight

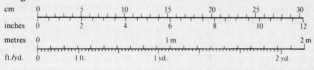

Length

COURTESIES. On entering and leaving a shop, restaurant or office, the expected greeting is *buon giorno* (good morning) or *buona sera* (good evening). When approaching anyone with an enquiry, the correct form is *per favore* (please), and for any service say *grazie* (thanks), to which the reply is *prego* (don't mention it; you're welcome).

Introductions are usually accompanied by handshaking and the phrase *piacere* (it's a pleasure). With people you know well, *ciao* is the casual form of greeting or farewell. When wished *buon appetito* before starting a meal, reply *grazie, altrettanto* (thank you, and the same to you).

How are you?	**Come sta?**
Very well, thanks.	**Molto bene, grazie.**

CRIME and THEFT. Petty theft is an endless annoyance, but cases of violence against tourists are rare. It's wise to leave unneeded documents and excess cash in the hotel safe and keep what you take in an inside pocket. Handbags are particularly vulnerable; agile thieves, often operating in pairs on motorscooters, whisk past and snatch them from your shoulder, sometimes even cutting or breaking the straps to do so. Be particularly attentive on crowded public transport or in secluded streets and districts. It's a good idea to make photocopies of your tickets, passport and other vital documents, to facilitate reporting any theft and obtaining replacements.

C

If you park your car, lock it and empty it of everything, leaving the glove compartments open to discourage prospective thieves.

I want to report a theft.	**Voglio denunciare un furto.**
My wallet/handbag/passport/ ticket has been stolen.	**Mi hanno rubato il portafoglio/ la borsa/il passaporto/ il biglietto.**

CUSTOMS (*dogana*) **and ENTRY REGULATIONS.** For a stay of up to three months, a valid passport is sufficient for citizens of Australia, Canada, New Zealand and U.S.A. Visitors from Eire and and the United Kingdom need only an identity card to enter Italy. Tourists from South Africa must have a visa.

Here are some main items you can take into Italy duty-free and, when returning home, into your own country:

Entering Italy from:	Cigarettes		Cigars		Tobacco	Spirits		Wine
1)	200	or	50	or	250 g.	1 l.	or	5 l.
2)	300	or	75	or	400 g.	¾ l.	and	2 l.
3)	400	or	100	or	500 g.	¾ l.	or	2 l.
Into:								
Australia	250	or	250 g.	or	250 g.	1 l.	or	1 l.
Canada	200	and	50	and	900 g.	1.1 l.	or	1.1 l.
Eire	200	or	50	or	250 g.	1 l.	and	2 l.
N. Zealand	200	or	50	or	250 g.	1.1 l.	and	4.5 l.
S. Africa	400	and	50	and	250 g.	1 l.	and	2 l.
U.K.	200	or	50	or	250 g.	1 l.	and	2 l.
U.S.A.	200	and	100	and	4)	1 l.	or	1 l.

1) Within Europe from non-EEC countries.
2) Within Europe from EEC countries.
3) Countries outside Europe.
4) A reasonable quantity.

Currency restrictions. As a foreign tourist, you may import unlimited amounts in local or other currencies, but to take more than L. 1,000,000 or the equivalent of more than L. 20,000,000 in foreign money out again, you must fill in a V2 declaration form at the border when you arrive.

If you're exporting archaeological relics, works of art or gems, you should obtain a bill of sale and a permit from the government (normally handled by the dealer).

I've nothing to declare.	**Non ho nullo da dichiarare.**
It's for my personal use.	**È per mio uso personale.**

DRIVING IN ITALY. To bring your car into Italy, you will need:

● an International Driving Permit or a valid national licence
● car registration papers
● Green Card (an extension to your regular insurance policy, making it valid specifically for Italy)
● a red warning triangle in case of breakdown
● national identity sticker for your car

Drivers of cars that are not their own must have the owner's written permission.

Before leaving home, check with your automobile association about the latest regulations concerning *petrol coupons* (giving tourists access to cheaper fuel) in Italy, as these are constantly changing.

Speed limits. Speed limits in Italy are based on the car engine size. The speed limit on motorways is 130 kph for cars with engines more powerful than 1,100 cubic centimetres. Less powerful cars cannot exceed 110 kph. On other roads the limit is 90 kph. These maximum speeds may be revised again. Ask at your automobile association before departure. The limit in built-up areas is usually 50 kph.

Driving conditions. Drive on the right, pass on the left. Traffic on major roads has right of way over that entering from side roads; this, like other traffic regulations, is frequently ignored, so be very careful. At intersections of roads of similar importance, the car on the right has the priority. When passing other vehicles, or remaining in the lefthand (passing) lane, keep your directional indicator flashing.

The motorways *(autostrada)* are designed for fast and safe driving; a toll is collected for each section. Take a card from an automatic machine or from the booth attendant and pay at the other end according to the distance travelled.

The use of seat-belts became obligatory in 1989.

Driving in Rome. Only the most intrepid motorist stays cool in the face of the Romans' hair-raising driving techniques. But, Roman drivers are not reckless—simply attuned to a different concept of driving. If you observe

D the following ground rules and venture with prudence into the urban traffic whirlpool, you stand a good chance of coming out unscathed.

Glance round to right and left and in your rear-view mirror all the time; other drivers are doing the same, and they've developed quick reflexes.

Treat traffic lights which are theoretically in your favour and white lines across merging side streets with caution—don't take your priority for granted.

To make progress in a traffic jam in one of Rome's squares, inch gently but confidently forward into the snarl-up. To wave on another driver, courteously letting him or her cut in ahead of you, is tantamount to abdicating your rights as a motorist.

Traffic-free zones are being tried out in various parts of town; these areas are constantly changing (but growing), and as at present, much of the city centre is "under trial".

Traffic police *(polizia stradale)*. All cities and many towns and villages have signs posted at the outskirts indicating the telephone number of the local traffic police or *carabinieri*.

The traffic police patrol the highways and byways on motorcycles or in Alfa Romeos, usually light blue. Speeding fines often have to be paid on the spot; ask for a receipt *(ricevuta)*.

Breakdowns. Call boxes are located at regular intervals on the *autostrade* in case of breakdowns or other emergencies. You can dial 116 for breakdown service from the ACI.

Fuel and oil. Service stations abound in Italy, usually with at least one mechanic on duty. Most stations close on Sundays, and every day from noon to 3 p.m. Fuel *(benzina)*, sold at government-set prices, comes in super (98–100 octane), unleaded—still rare—(95 octane) and normal (86–88 octane). Diesel fuel is usually also available.

Fluid measures

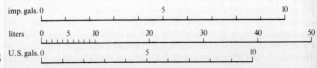

114

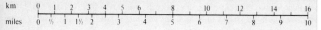

Distance **D**

Parking (see also CRIME AND THEFT). For motorized tourists as well residents, parking is one of Rome's greatest challenges. Your wisest course is to find a legal parking place near your hotel for the duration of your stay and see the city on foot or by public transport.

There are formal guarded parking areas operated by the ACI; they are not watched overnight. And Rome has a raft of freelance parking attendants who will offer to "guard" your car, even if illegally parked, for a fee.

Beware particularly of tow-away zones; if you park your car there, it may be towed to the municipal garages or parking lots. To retrieve it, you first have to go to the municipal police *(vigili urbani)* to find out where it has been taken. You then collect your car—and a hefty fine. On Sundays and public holidays the municipal garages are closed and cars cannot be recovered.

Road signs. Most road signs employed in Italy are international pictographs, but there are some written ones you may come across:

Accendere le luci	Use headlights
Deviazione	Diversion (Detour)
Divieto di sorpasso	No overtaking (passing)
Divieto di sosta	No stopping
Lavori in corso	Road works (Men working)
Passaggio a livello	Level railway crossing
Pericolo	Danger
Rallentare	Slow down
Senso unico	One-way street
Senso vietato/Vietato l'ingresso	No entry
Zona pedonale	Pedestrian zone

driving licence	**patente**
car registration papers	**libretto di circolazione**
green card	**carta verde**
Fill the tank, please.	**Per favore, faccia il pieno.**
super/normal	**super/normale**
unleaded/diesel	**senza piombo/gasolio**
I've had a breakdown.	**Ho avuto un guasto.**
There's been an accident.	**C'è stato un incidente.**

E **ELECTRICITY.** Generally 220 volts, 50 Hz AC, but sometimes 125volt outlets, with different plugs and sockets for each. The voltage might be indicated on the socket in hotels, but it's best to ask, to avoid ruining your shaver or hair dryer.

EMERGENCIES. In an emergency you can phone the following numbers 24 hours a day:

Police, all purpose emergency number	113
Carabinieri (see POLICE) for urgent police problems	112
Fire	115
Ambulance and Red Cross	51 00
Night and day medical service	4756741
Road assistance (ACI) and advice for tourists	116

Careful!	**Attenzione!**
Fire!	**Incendio!**
Help!	**Aiuto!**
Stop thief!	**Al ladro!**

G **GUIDES and TOURS.** Most hotels in Rome can arrange for multilingual guides or interpreters. A selection is found in the yellow pages of the telephone directory under the entry "Traduzione", and local newspapers carry advertisements offering such services. There are also guides near most of the major tourist attractions, and portable recorders with commentaries in English can often be hired.

CIT and many private firms offer tours of all the major sights, plus excursions to other points of interest. Often tourists are picked up and dropped off at their hotels. Your hotel receptionist will have a list of available guided group tours.

H **HAIRDRESSERS and BARBERS** *(parrucchiere; barbiere).* Women should telephone in advance for an appointment. As in most countries, the owner of a salon should never be tipped; the shampooist, manicurist or stylist should be tipped up to 15% of the bill.

I'd like a shampoo and set.	**Vorrei shampo e messa in piega.**
I want a...	**Voglio...**
haircut	**il taglio**
shave	**la rasatura**
blow-dry (brushing)	**asciugatura al fon**
permanent wave	**la permanente**

HEALTH and MEDICAL CARE. If your health-insurance policy does
not cover foreign countries, take out a short-term policy before leaving
home. Visitors from Great Britain and Ireland, as members of the EEC,
can claim public health services available to Italians. Before departure
obtain a copy of the proper form (E 111) from the U.K. Department of
Health and Social Security.

If you need medical care, ask your hotel receptionist to help you find a
doctor (or dentist) who speaks English. Both the U.S. and British
embassies (see p. 110) have lists of English-speaking doctors. Local
Health Units of the Italian National Health Service are listed in the telephone directory under "Unità Sanitaria Locale". The first-aid *(pronto soc-
corso)* section of hospitals handles medical emergencies.

Pharmacies. The Italian *farmacia* is open during shopping hours (see
HOURS). Usually one operates at night and on weekends for each district
on a rota basis. The opening schedule for duty pharmacies is posted on
every pharmacy door and in the local papers.

Bring along an adequate supply of any prescribed medication.

I need a doctor/dentist.	**Ho bisogno di un medico/**
	dentista.
Where's the nearest (all-	**Dov'è la farmacia (di turno) più**
night) chemist?	**vicina?**

HOURS. Even within Rome opening hours vary. In true Mediterranean
fashion, much of the city shuts or slows down after lunch. However, for
some offices the modern non-stop business day is gradually creeping in.
The following therefore is just a guideline.

Shops. Open 8.30 a.m.–1 p.m. and 5–8 p.m. (summer hours), Monday to
Saturday (half-day closing is usually Monday mornings); food stores open
8.30 a.m.–12.30 or 1 p.m. and 5–7.30 p.m. (half-day closing usually
Thursday afternoons). Tourist resort shops stay open all day, every day, in
high season.

Post offices. Normally open 8.30 a.m.–2 p.m., Monday to Friday, until
noon on Saturdays. The main post office in Piazza San Silvestro and the
branch at Stazione Termini stay open till 7.45 p.m.

Banks. 8.30 a.m.–1.30 p.m. and again for an hour or so in the afternoon,
Monday to Friday.

Principal businesses. 8 or 9 a.m.–1 or 1.30 p.m. and 4, 4.30 or 5–7, 7.30
or 8 p.m., Monday to Saturday. Sometimes closed Saturday afternoons.

Pharmacies. Open 8.30 a.m.–1 p.m. and 4–8 p.m.

H **Museums and historic sites.** These are usually open Tuesday to Sunday, from 9 a.m. to 2 p.m. (if not earlier), and, in some cases, also from 5 to 8 p.m. Closing day is usually Monday; if Monday is a holiday, the museums are closed the following day.

L **LANGUAGE.** Italians appreciate foreigners making an effort to speak their language, even if only a few words. In the major tourist hotels and shops, staff usually speak some English.

Remember that the letter "c" is pronounced like "ch" when it is followed by an "e" or an "i", while the letters "ch" together sound like the "c" in cat.

The Berlitz phrase book ITALIAN FOR TRAVELLERS covers most situations you are likely to encounter; also useful is the Italian-English/English-Italian pocket dictionary, with a special menu-reader supplement.

Do you speak English?	**Parla inglese?**
I don't speak Italian.	**Non parlo italiano.**

LAUNDRY and DRY-CLEANING. Most hotels handle laundry and dry-cleaning. For lower rates you can do your own washing at a *lavanderia* (or leave it with the attendant) or hand it in at a *tintoria,* which usually offers a normal or express service. Most hotels will handle laundry and dry-cleaning, but rates are much higher.

When will it be ready?	**Quando sarà pronto?**
I must have this for tomorrow morning.	**Mi serve per domani mattina.**

LOST PROPERTY. Cynics say anything lost in Italy is lost forever, but that's not necessarily true in Rome. Restaurants more often than not will have your forgotten briefcase, guide book or camera waiting for you at the cashier's desk. If you've lost something away from your hotel, go to the lost property office *(Ufficio Oggetti Rinvenuti)*

Via Bettoni, 1; tel. 5816040.
There are lost property offices at the Termini railway station (tel. 4730/6682) and at ATAC in Via Volturno, 65; tel. 4695. For losses on the metro, phone 57 351.

Report lost documents to the police or your consulate.

I've lost my passport/wallet/ handbag.	**Ho perso il passaporto/ portafoglio/la borsetta.**

MAPS *(pianta).* Newsstands and tourist offices have a large selection of maps at a wide range of prices. Some are old (look for the publication date in a corner of the map), and others may have pretty symbols of the Colosseum and St. Peter's, but hopelessly distort urban proportions. The maps in this guide were prepared by Falk-Verlag, Hamburg, which also publishes a complete map to Italy and to Rome.

MONEY MATTERS (see also HOURS)

Currency. The *lira* (plural: *lire,* abbreviated *L.* or *Lit.*) is Italy's monetary unit.

Coins: L. 5, 10, 20, 50, 100, 200 and 500.

Notes: L. 1,000, 2,000, 5,000, 10,000, 50,000 and 100,000.

For currency restrictions, see CUSTOMS AND ENTRY REGULATIONS.

Currency exchange offices *(cambio)* are usually open from 9 a.m. to 1.30 p.m. and 2.30 to 6 p.m. Many are closed on Saturdays. Exchange rates are less advantageous than in banks. A flat rate of commission is common, so it is not worth changing small amounts many times. Passports are sometimes required when changing money.

Credit cards and traveller's cheques. Most hotels, many shops and some restaurants take credit cards. Traveller's cheques are accepted almost everywhere, but you will get better value if you exchange your cheques for lire at a bank or *cambio.* Passports are required when cashing cheques. Eurocheques are fairly easily cashed in Italy.

I want to change some pounds/ dollars.	**Desidero cambiare delle sterline/ dei dollari.**
Do you accept traveller's cheques?	**Accetta traveller's cheques?**
Can I pay with this credit card?	**Posso pagare con la carta di credito?**

NEWSPAPERS AND MAGAZINES. Some British and continental newspapers and magazines are on sale, sometimes a day late, at the airport and stations and in the kiosks. The *International Herald Tribune* is printed in Rome and is available early in the morning. Prices are high for all foreign publications.

Have you any English-language newspapers?	**Avete giornali in inglese?**

P **POLICE.** The municipal police *(Vigili Urbani)*, dressed in navy blue with white helmets or all-white with shiny buttons, handle city traffic and other city police tasks. They are courteous and helpful to tourists, though they rarely speak a foreign language. Those who act as interpreters carry a badge.

The *carabinieri*—who wear dark blue uniforms with a red stripe down the side of the trousers—deal with theft, more serious crimes, demonstrations and military affairs. The national, or state, police *(polizia di stato)* are distinguished by their dark blue jackets and light blue trousers, and handle other police and administrative matters. (For traffic police see DRIVING IN ITALY.)

The all-purpose emergency number, 113, will get you police help.

Where's the nearest police station? | **Dov'è il più vicino posto di polizia?**

PUBLIC HOLIDAYS *(festa)*. When a national holiday falls on a Thursday or a Tuesday, Italians may make a *ponte* (bridge) to the weekend, meaning that Friday or Monday is taken off as well.

January 1	*Capodanno* or *Primo dell'Anno*	New Year's Day
January 6	*Epifania*	Epiphany
April 25	*Fiesta della Liberazione*	Liberation Day
May 1	*Festa del Lavoro*	Labour Day
August 25	*Ferragosto*	Assumption Day
November 1	*Ognissanti*	All Saints' Day
December 8	*L'Immacolata Concezione*	Immaculate Conception
December 25	*Natale*	Christmas Day
December 26	*Santo Stefano*	St. Stephen's Day
Movable date: *Lundi di Pasqua*		Easter Monday

Note: On all national holidays, banks, government offices, most shops and some museums and galleries are closed.

R **RADIO AND TV** *(radio; televisione)*. The Italian state radio and TV network is the RAI. During the tourist season, RAI radio broadcasts news in **120** English from Monday to Saturday at 10 a.m. and on Sundays at 9.30 a.m.

Vatican Radio carries foreign-language religious news programmes. British (BBC), American (VOA) and Canadian (CBC) programmes are easily obtained on short-wave transistor radios. RAI television and private channels broadcast only in Italian, although you can pick up the CBS television news from the previous evening twice each morning from Tuesdays to Saturday.

RELIGIOUS SERVICES. Roman Catholic mass is celebrated daily and several times on Sunday in Italian. Some services are in English. Major non-Catholic denominations and Jews have congregations in Rome, often with services in English.

Mass is celebrated in St. Peter's Basilica every day. On Sundays, there is high mass at 10.30 a.m. and 4 p.m., with vespers at 5 p.m. On other days, continuous mass is at 7–9 a.m., 10 a.m., 11 a.m. and 12 noon. Pilgrims' mass is held on Thursdays at 9 a.m.

TIME DIFFERENCES. Italy follows Central European Time (GMT + 1), and from late March to September clocks are put one hour ahead (GMT + 2). Summer time chart:

NewYork	London	**Italy**	Jo'burg	Sydney	Auckland
6a.m.	11a.m.	**noon**	noon	8p.m.	10p.m.

What time is it?   **Che ore sono?**

TIPPING. A service charge is added to most restaurant bills, but it is customary to leave an additional tip. It is also in order to tip bellboys, doormen, hat check attendants, garage attendants, etc. The chart below will give you some guidelines:

Hotel porter, per bag	L.1,000
Hotel maid, per day	L. 1,000–2,000
Lavatory attendant	L. 300
Waiter	5–10%
Taxi driver	10%
Hairdresser/Barber	up to 15%
tour guide	10%

TOILETS. Most museums and art galleries have public toilets. Bars, restaurants, cafés, large stores, the airports, railway stations and car parks

T all have facilities. On the whole they are clean and in good order, but carry your own tissues.

Toilets may be labelled with a symbol of a man or a woman or the initials W.C. Sometimes the wording will be in Italian, but beware, as you might be misled: *Uomini* is for men, *Donne* is for women. Equally, *Signori*—with a final *i*—is for men, *Signore*—with a final *e*—is for women.

Where are the toilets? **Dove sono i gabinetti?**

TOURIST INFORMATION OFFICES. The Italian Tourist Office *(Ente Nazionale Italiano per il Turismo,* abbreviated ENIT) is represented in Italy and abroad. They publish detailed brochures with up-to-date information on accommodation, means of transport and other general tips and useful addresses for the whole country.

Australia and New Zealand	c/o Italian Government Tourist Office, Lion's Building, 1-1-2 Moto Akasaka, Minato-Ku, Tokyo 107; tel. (3) 478 2051
Canada	1, Place Ville-Marie, Suite 1914, Montreal H3B 3M9, Que.; tel. (514) 866.76.67.
Eire	47, Merrion Square, Dublin; tel. (3531) 766 397.
South Africa	ENIT, P.O. Box 6507, Johannesburg 2000.
United Kingdom	1, Princes Street, London W1R 8AY; tel. (01) 408 1254.
U.S.A.	500 N. Michigan Avenue, Suite 1046, Chicago, Il 60611; tel. (312) 6440990/1. 630 Fifth Avenue, Suite 1565, New York, NY 10111; tel. (212) 245-4961. 360 Post Street, Suite 801, San Francisco, CA 94108; tel. (415) 3925266.

The tourist office headquarters in Rome are at

Via Parigi, 11; tel. 488 1851
Via Parigi, 5 (Tourist Assistance); tel. 488 3748, with branches at Stazione Termini and Fiumicino airport.

122 Where's the tourist office? **Dov'è l'ufficio turistico?**

Underground/Subway (*metropolitana,* or *metrò*). Rome has two underground railway lines. Line A runs from Via Ottaviano near the Vatican south-east to Via Anagnina, stopping at more than 20 stations and passing under most of Rome's popular tourist sights. The intersecting Line B runs from Rebibbia via Termini railway station and Piramide to Eur Fermi. From there, you can take a metro train which leaves every 30 minutes for Ostia Lido. Entrances are marked by a large red *M*. Tickets are sold at newsstands and tobacconists, or can be purchased from machines at the stations.

Buses (*autobus*). Rome's fleet of orange buses serves every corner of the city. Although crowded on certain routes and at rush hours, they are an inexpensive way of crossing the city. Newsstands sell maps showing the major bus routes. Each bus stop (*fermata*) indicates the numbers and times of the buses stopping there and the routes they serve. Tickets for buses must be bought in advance from newsstands or tobacco shops. Enter by the rear doors and punch your ticket in a machine; exit by the middle doors. Tickets are time-based: 1 ½ hours, 1 day, 7 days, and one month. They are available from offices of Rome's public transport organization (ATAC) at Largo Giovanni Montemartini and Piazza dei Cinquecento, both near Stazione Termini.

ACOTRAL [tel. (06) 591-5551] operates bus services to the environs of Rome.

Taxis (*tassì* or *taxi*). The distinctive yellow taxis may be hailed in the street (but vacant ones are hard to find), picked up at a taxi rank or obtained by telephone. The yellow pages of the telephone directory list all the ranks under "Taxi".

Taxis remain cheap by North European and American standards, but make sure that the meter is running. Extra charges for luggage and for night, holiday or airport trips are posted in four languages inside all taxis. A tip of at least 10% is customary. Beware of the non-metered unlicensed taxis (*"abusivi"*), which charge much more than the normal taxi rates for trips in private cars.

Radio-Taxi, phone 3570/4994/8433

Horse-cabs (*carrozza*). A familiar sight in Rome for centuries, horse-drawn carriages now, sadly, number only a few dozen. Found at tourist haunts such as St. Peter's Square, the Spanish Steps and the Colisseum, the horse-cabs theoretically have meters, but it's best to agree a price with the driver before setting off.

T **Train.** The Italian State Railway *(Ferrovie dello Stato)* operates an extensive network all over the country. The fares are among the lowest in Europe. Choose your train carefully, as journey times vary a good deal. The following list describes the various types of train:

Eurocity (EC)	International express; first and second class; surcharge on many.
Intercity (IC)/ Rapido	High-speed super-express; first class only (ticket includes seat reservation, newspaper, refreshments). Also first and second class; stops at main stations; surcharge.
Expresso (Expr.)	Long-distance train, stopping at main stations.
Diretto (Dir.)	Slower than the *Expresso*, it makes a number of local stops.
Locale (L)	Local train which stops at almost every station.
Metropolitana (servizi dedicati)	Connecting service from airports and sea ports to major cities.

Children between 4 and 12 years of age pay half fare. See also p. 104 for special offers.

Tickets can be purchased and reservations made at a local travel agency or at the railway station. Better-class trains have dining-cars or self-service cars which offer food and beverages at reasonable prices. If you don't have a reservation, you should arrive at the station at least 20 minutes before departure; Italy's trains are often crowded.

Where's the nearest bus stop/ underground station?	**Dov'è la fermata d'autobus/la stazione della metropolitana più vicina?**
When's the next bus/ train to…?	**Quando parte il prossimo autobus/treno per…?**
I'd like a ticket to…	**Vorrei un biglietto per…**
single (one-way)	**andata**
return (round-trip)	**andata e ritorno**

WATER. Rome's drinking water, not least from its outdoor fountains, is famous for its flavour and is perfectly safe. Nonetheless, with meals it is customary to drink bottled mineral water. If tap water is not drinkable it will usually carry a sign reading *acqua non potabile*.

I'd like a bottle of mineral water.	**Vorrei una bottiglia di acqua minerale.**
fizzy (carbonated)/still	**gasata/naturale**

SOME USEFUL EXPRESSIONS

yes/no	**sì/no**
please/thank you	**per favore/grazie**
excuse me/you're welcome	**mi scusi/prego**
where/when/how	**dove/quando/come**
how long/how far	**quanto tempo/quanto dista**
yesterday/today/tomorrow	**ieri/oggi/domani**
day/week/month/year	**giorno/settimana/mese/anno**
left/right	**sinistra/destra**
up/down	**su/giù**
good/bad	**buono/cattivo**
big/small	**grande/piccolo**
cheap/expensive	**buon mercato/caro**
hot/cold	**caldo/freddo**
open/closed	**aperto/chiuso**
free (vacant)/occupied	**liberto/occupato**
near/far	**vicino/lontano**
early/late	**presto/tardi**
right/wrong	**guisto/sbagliato**
I don't understand.	**Non capisco.**
Waiter/Waitress, please.	**Cameriere!/Cameriera!** (or **Senta!** = "listen")
I'd like…	**Vorrei…**
How much is that?	**Quant'è?**

Index

An asterisk (*) next to a page number indicates a map reference. Where there is more than one set of page references, the one in bold type refers to the main entry.

INDEX

Selection of Rome Hotels and Restaurants

Where do you start? Choosing an hotel or restaurant in a place you're not familiar with can be daunting. To help you find your way in Rome, we have made a selection from the *Red Guide to Italy* published by Michelin, the recognized authority on gastronomy and accommodation throughout Europe.

Our own Berlitz criteria have been price and location. In the hotel section, for a double room with bath and breakfast, Higher-priced means above L. 300,000, Medium-priced L. 150,000–300,000, Lower-priced below L. 150,000. As to restaurants, for a meal consisting of a starter, a main course and a dessert, Higher-priced means above L. 60,000, Medium-priced L. 40,000–60,000, Lower-priced below L. 40,000. Special features where applicable, plus regular closing days are also given. As a general rule many Rome restaurants are closed in August. For hotels and restaurants, both a check to make certain that they are open and advance reservations are advisable.

For a wider choice of hotels and restaurants, we recommend you obtain the Michelin *Red Guide to Italy,* which gives a comprehensive and reliable picture of the situation throughout the country.

Note that, owing to modernisation of the Italian telephone system, telephone numbers in Rome can change at short notice.

HOTELS

HIGHER-PRICED

(above L. 300,000)

Aldrovandi Palace Hotel
via Aldrovandi 15
00197 Rome
Tel. 322 3993; fax 3221435
139 rooms
*Outdoor swimming pool.
Garden.*

Ambasciatori Palace
via Vittorio Veneto 70
00187 Rome
Tel. 47493; fax 474 3601
150 rooms
Grill Bar ABC restaurant.

Atlante Garden
via Crescenzio 78/a
00193 Rome
Tel. 687 2361; fax 687 2315
43 rooms

Atlante Star
via Vitelleschi 34
00193 Rome
Tel. 687 9558; fax 687 23500
61 rooms
*Roof-garden restaurant with
view over St. Peter's Basilica.*

Cavalieri Hilton
via Cadlolo 101
00136 Rome
Tel. 31511; fax 31 51 2241
374 rooms
*Quiet hotel. View of the city.
Terrace and park. Outdoor
swimming pool. Hotel tennis
court.*

D'Inghilterra
via Bocca di Leone 14
00187 Rome
Tel. 672161; fax 684 0828
105 rooms
No restaurant.

Eden
via Ludovisi 49
00187 Rome
Tel. 4743551; fax 474 2401
110 rooms
*Roof-garden restaurant with
view over city.*

Forum
Tor de' Conti 28
00184 Rome
Tel. 679 2446; fax 679 9337
76 rooms
*Roof-garden restaurant
with view of
Imperial Forums.*

Giulio Cesare
via degli Scipioni 287
00192 Rome
Tel. 321 0751; fax 321 1736
86 rooms
Garden. No restaurant.

Hassler
piazza Trinità dei Monti 6
00187 Rome
Tel. 679 2651; fax 678 9991
103 rooms
*View over city from roof-garden
restaurant.*

Jolly Vittorio Veneto
corso d'Italia 1
00198 Rome
Tel. 8495; fax 680 8457
203 rooms

Le Grand Hotel
via Vittorio Emanuele Orlando 3
00185 Rome
Tel. 4709; fax 474 7307
171 rooms

Lord Byron
via De Notaris 5
00197 Rome
Tel. 322 0404; fax 322 0405
47 rooms
Quiet, pleasant hotel. Garden.

Outskirts of Rome

Sheraton
viale del Pattinaggio
00144 Rome
Tel. 5453; fax 542 3281
587 rooms
Outdoor swimming pool. Hotel tennis court.

MEDIUM-PRICED
(L. 150,000–300,000)

Accademia
piazza Accademia
di San Luca 75
00187 Rome
Tel. 678 6705; fax 678 5897
55 rooms
No restaurant.

Albani
via Adda 45
00198 Rome
Tel. 8499; fax 849 9399
157 rooms
No restaurant.

Arcangelo
via Boezio 15
00192 Rome
Tel. 689 6459; fax 689 3050
30 rooms
No restaurant.

Borromini
via Lisbona 7
00198 Rome
Tel. 884 1321; fax 841 7550
75 rooms
No restaurant.

Britannia
via Napoli 64
00184 Rome
Tel. 488 5785; fax 488 2343
32 rooms
No restaurant.

Clodio
via di Santa Lucia 10
00195 Rome
Tel. 317541; fax 325 0745
114 rooms
No restaurant.

Colonna Palace
piazza Montecitorio 12
00186 Rome
Tel. 678 1341; fax 679 4496
105 rooms
No restaurant.

Columbus
via della Conciliazione 33
00193 Rome
Tel. 686 5435; fax 686 5245
107 rooms
15th-century-style building.
Garden.

Commodore
via Torino 1
00184 Rome
Tel. 485656; fax 474 7562
60 rooms
No restaurant.

Degli Aranci
via B. Oriani 11
00197 Rome
Tel. 808 5250
42 rooms
Outdoor dining.

Diana
via Principe Amedeo 4
00185 Rome
Tel. 482 7541; fax 486998
187 rooms

Diplomatic
via Vittorio Colonna 28
00193 Rome
Tel. 687 4372; fax 683 2685
40 rooms
Outdoor dining.

Edera
via Poliziano 75
00184 Rome
Tel. 731 6341; fax 738275
48 rooms
Quiet hotel with garden. No
restaurant.

Eliseo
via di Porta Pinciana 30
00187 Rome
Tel. 487 0456
Tlx. 481 9729
53 rooms
Roof-garden restaurant with
view of Villa Borghese.

Fenix
viale Gorizia 5
00198 Rome
Tel. 854 9786; fax 854 3632
69 rooms
Garden.

Genova
via Cavour 33
00184 Rome
Tel. 476951; fax 482 7580
91 rooms
No restaurant.

Gregoriana
via Gregoriana 18
00187 Rome
Tel. 679 4269
19 rooms
No restaurant.

Imperiale
via Vittorio Veneto 24
00187 Rome
Tel./Fax 482 6351
85 rooms

Internazionale
via Sistina 79
00187 Rome
Tel. 679 3047 9Fax 678 4794
39 rooms
No restaurant.

Jolly Leonardo da Vinci
via dei Gracchi 324
00192 Rome
Tel. 324499; fax 361 0138
272 rooms

King
via Sistina 131
00187 Rome
Tel. 474 1515; fax 491047
79 rooms
No restaurant.

Madrid
via Mario de' Fiori 89
00187 Rome
Tel. 684 0998; fax 679 1653
24 rooms
No restaurant.

Massimo D'Azeglio
via Cavour 18
00184 Rome
Tel. 487 0270; fax 482 7386
210 rooms

Mediterraneo
via Cavour 15
00184 Rome
Tel. 488 4051; fax 474 4105
272 rooms

Mozart
via dei Greci 23/b
00187 Rome
Tel. 678 7422; fax 678 4271
31 rooms
No restaurant.

Napoleon
piazza Vittorio Emanuele 105
00185 Rome
Tel. 737646; fax 731 1202
80 rooms

Nord-Nuova Roma
via Amendola 3
00185 Rome
Tel. 488 5441; fax 481 7163
156 rooms
No restaurant.

Quirinale
via Nazionale 7
00184 Rome
Tel. 4707; fax 482 0099
186 rooms
Outdoor dining. Garden.

Regency
via Romagna 42
00187 Rome
Tel. 481 9281; fax 481 9091
50 rooms
No restaurant.

Rivoli
via Torquato Taramelli 7
00197 Rome
Tel. 322 4042; fax 322 7373
54 rooms

San Giorgio
via Amendola 61
00185 Rome
Tel. 482 7341; fax 488 3191
186 rooms
No restaurant.

Siena
via Sant'Andrea delle Frate 33
00187 Rome
Tel. 679 6121; fax 678 7509
21 rooms
No restaurant.

Sitea
via Vittorio Emanuele Orlando 90
00185 Rome
Tel. 482 7560; fax 481 7637
37 rooms
No restaurant.

Victoria
via Campania 41
00187 Rome
Tel. 473931; fax 487 1890
110 rooms

Villa del Parco
via Nomentana 110
00161 Rome
Tel. 855 4115; fax 854 0410
23 rooms
Garden. No restaurant.

Visconti Palace
via Federico Cesi 37
00193 Rome
Tel. 3684; fax 320 0551
247 rooms
No restaurant.

Outskirts of Rome

Dei Congressi
viale Shakespeare 29
00144 Rome
Tel. 592 1264; fax 591 1903
96 rooms
No restaurant.

Holiday Inn St. Peter's
via Aurelia Antica 415
00165 Rome
Tel. 5872; fax 663 7190
336 rooms
*Outdoor swimming pool.
Garden. Hotel tennis court.*

Holiday Inn-Eur Parco dei Medici
viale Castello della Magliana 65
00148 Rome
Tel. 65581; fax 655 7005
331 rooms
*Outdoor swimming pool.
Garden. Hotel tennis court.*

Villa Pamphili
via della Nocetta 105
00164 Rome
Tel. 5862; fax 625 7747
257 rooms
Outdoor swimming pool (covered in winter). Garden. Hotel tennis court.

LOWER-PRICED
(below L. 150,000)

Alba
via Leonina 12
00184 Rome
Tel. 484712; fax 488 4840
26 rooms
No restaurant.

Alpi
via Castelfidardo 84/a
00185 Rome
Tel. 44412; fax 444 1257
46 rooms
No restaurant.

Ariston
via F. Turati 16
00185 Rome
Tel. 446 5397
97 rooms
No restaurant.

Canada
via Vicenza 58
00185 Rome
Tel. 445 7770; fax 445 0749
62 rooms
No restaurant.

Colosseum
via Sforza 10
00184 Rome
Tel. 482 7228; fax 4827285
50 rooms
No restaurant.

Della Conciliazione
borgo Pio 164
00193 Rome
Tel. 686 7910; fax 6541164
55 rooms
No restaurant.

Della Torre Argentina
corso Vittorio Emanuele 102
00186 Rome
Tel. 683 3886; fax 654 1641
32 rooms
No restaurant.

Diana
via Principe Amedeo 4
00185 Rome
Tel. 482 7541; fax 486998
187 rooms

Domus Maximi
via Santa Prisca 11/b
00153 Rome
Tel. 5782565
23 rooms
Quiet hotel.

Eurogarden
raccordo anulare SalariaFlaminia
00138 Rome
Tel./Fax 880 4417
40 rooms
Outdoor swimming pool.
Garden. No restaurant.

Galileo
via Palestro 33
00185 Rome
Tel. 404 1205; fax 4041208
38 rooms
No restaurant.

Gerber
via degli Scipioni 241
00192 Rome
Tel. 321 6485; fax 3217048
27 rooms
No restaurant.

Lloyd
via Alessandria 110
00198 Rome
Tel. 854 0432; fax 841 9846
48 rooms
No restaurant.

Lux Messe
via Volturno 32
00185 Rome
Tel. 474 1741; fax 482 8302
99 rooms
No restaurant.

Margutta
via Laurina 34
00187 Rome
Tel. 322 3674
21 rooms
No restaurant.

Milani
via Magenta 12
00185 Rome
Tel. 445 7051; fax 446 2317
76 rooms
No restaurant.

Portoghesi
via dei Portoghesi 1
00186 Rome
Tel. 686 4231; fax 654 5133
27 rooms
No restaurant.

Sant'Anselmo
piazza Sant'Anselmo 2
00153 Rome
Tel. 574 3547; fax 578 3604
45 rooms
Garden. No restaurant.

Senato
piazza della Rotonda 73
00186 Rome
Tel. 679 3231; fax 684 0297
51 rooms
*View of the Pantheon. No
restaurant.*

Siviglia
via Gaeta 12
00185 Rome
Tel. 441 1197; fax 444 1195
40 rooms
No restaurant.

Villa Florence
via Nomentana 28
00161 Rome
Tel. 440 3036; fax 440 2709
33 rooms
Garden. No restaurant.

Villa San Pio
Piazza Sant'Anselmo 2
00153 Rome
Tel. 574 5231; fax 578 3674
59 rooms
Garden. No restaurant.

RESTAURANTS

HIGHER-PRICED
(above L. 60,000)

Al Moro
vicolo delle Bollete 13
00187 Rome Tel. 678 3495
*Trattoria. Reservation essential.
Closed Sunday.*

Alberto Ciarla
piazza San Cosimato 40
00153 Rome
Tel. 588 4377; fax 688 4377
*Notably good cuisine. Outdoor
dining. Reservation essential.
Closed at lunchtime and Sunday.*

4 Colonne
via della Posta 4
00186 Rome
Tel. 654 7152
*Reservation essential. Closed
Sunday.*

Coriolano
via Ancona 14
00198 Rome
Tel. 855 1122
Popular restaurant, reservation essential.
Closed Sunday.

El Toulà
via della Lupa 29/b
00186 Rome
Tel. 687 3498; fax 687 1115
Elegant restaurant.
Reservation essential.
Closed Saturday lunchtime and Sunday.

Girarrosto Toscano
via Campania 29
00187 Rome
Tel. 482 1899
Modern taverna.
Closed Wednesday.

Harry's Bar
via Vittorio Veneto 150
00187 Rome
Tel. 474 5832
Popular restaurant, reservation essential.
Closed Sunday.

La Maiella
piazza Sant'Apollinare 45/46
00186 Rome
Tel. 686 4174
Abruzzi specialities.
Outdoor dining.
Closed Sunday.

La Rosetta
via della Rosetta 9
00187 Rome
Tel. 686 1002
Trattoria with seafood specialities.
Notably good cuisine. Closed Sunday and Monday lunchtime.

Loreto
via Valenziani 19
00187 Rome
Tel. 474 5286
Seafood specialities.
Closed Sunday.

Patrizia e Roberto del Pianeta Terra
via Arco del Monte 94
00186 Rome
Tel. 686 9893
Elegant restaurant. Reservation essential. Notably good cuisine.

Piperno
Monte de' Cenci 9
00186 Rome
Tel. 654 0629
Roman specialities.

Ranieri
via Mario de' Fiori 26
00187 Rome
Tel. 679 1592
Reservation essential.
Closed Sunday.

Relais le Jardin
via De Notaris 5
00197 Rome
Tel. 322 0404; fax 322 0405
Excellent cuisine. Elegant restaurant. Reservation essential. Closed Sunday.

Sabatini
vicolo Santa Maria
in Trastevere 18
00153 Rome
Tel. 581 8307
*Outdoor dining. Seafood and
Roman specialities.
Closed Wednesday.*

**Sabatini a Santa Maria in
Trastevere**
piazza di Santa Maria
in Trastevere 13
00153 Rome
Tel. 581 2026
*Outdoor dining. Seafood and Roman
specialities. Closed Wednesday*

Sans Souci
via Sicilia 20
00187 Rome
Tel. 482 1814
*Notably good cuisine. Reservation
essential. Late-night dinners.
Closed at lunchtime and Monday.*

Squalo Bianco
via Federico Cesi 36
00193 Rome
Tel. 321 4700
Seafood specialities. Closed Sunday.

MEDIUM-PRICED
(L. 40,000–60,000)

Al 59-da Guiseppe
via Brunetti 59
00186 Rome
Tel. 321 9019
*Bolognese specialities. Closed
Sunday*

Al Ceppo
via Panama 2
00198 Rome
Tel. 841 9696
*Typical restaurant. Outdoor
dining. Closed Monday.*

Al Chianti
via Ancona 17
00198 Rome
Tel. 861083
*Tuscan trattoria with taverna.
Reservation essential. Closed
Sunday.*

Al Fogher
via Tevere 13/b
00198 Rome
Tel. 857032
*Typical restaurant with Venetian
specialities. Closed Sunday.*

Angelino ai Fori
largo Corrado Ricci 40
00184 Rome
Tel. 679 1121
Outdoor dining. Closed Tuesday.

Apuleius
via Tempio di Diana 15
00153 Rome
Tel. 574 2160
*Ancient-Roman-style taverna.
Closed Sunday.*

Cesarina
via Piemonte 109
00187 Rome
Tel. 488 0828
*Bolognese specialities. Closed
Sunday.*

Checco er Carettiere
via Benedetta 10
00153 Rome
Tel. 581 7018
*Outdoor dining, with seafood
and Roman specialities. Closed
Sunday evening and Monday.*

Colline Emiliane
via degli Avignonesi 22
00187 Rome
Tel. 481 7538
Reserve. Closed Friday.

Corsetti-il Galeone
piazza San Cosimato 27
00153 Rome
Tel. 581 6311
*Seafood specialities. Typical
atmosphere. Closed Wednesday.*

Da Benito
via Flaminia Nuova 230/232
00191 Rome
Tel. 327 2752
Closed Monday.

Da Giggetto
via del Portico d'Ottavia 21/a
00186 Rome
Tel. 686 1105
*Typical trattoria with Roman
specialities. Closed Monday.
Outdoor dining.*

Da Mario
via della Vite 56
00187 Rome
Tel. 678 3818
*Tuscan specialities. Closed
Sunday.*

Da Pancrazio
piazza del Biscione 92
00186 Rome
Tel. 686 1246
*On the foundations of Pompey's
Theatre.
Closed Wednesday.*

Da Severino
piazza Zama 5/c
00183 Rome
Tel. 700 0872
*Closed Sunday evening and all
day Monday.*

Dai Toscani
via Forli 41
00161 Rome
Tel. 883 1302
*Tuscan specialities.
Closed Sunday.*

Delle Vittorie
via Monte Santo 62/64
00195 Rome
Tel. 386847
Closed Sunday.

Eau Vive
via Monterone 85
00186 Rome
Tel. 654 1095
*16th-century building. Catholic
missionaries.
International cuisine.
Reservation essential in evening.
Closed Sunday.*

Er Comparone
piazza in Piscinula 47
00153 Rome
Tel. 581 6249
*Typical restaurant. Roman
specialities. Outdoor dining.
Closed Monday.*

Galeassi
piazza di Santa Maria
in Trastevere 3
00153 Rome
Tel. 580 3775
*Outdoor dining. Seafood and
Roman specialities. Closed
Monday.*

Giovanni
via Marche 64
00187 Rome
Tel. 482 1834
*Typical habitués' restaurant.
Closed Friday evening and
Saturday.*

Hostaria Costa Balena
via Messina 5/7
00198 Rome
Tel. 841 7686
*Trattoria with seafood
specialities. Closed Saturday
lunchtime and all day Sunday.*

Hostaria da Cesare
via Crescenzio 13
00193 Rome
Tel. 686 1227
*Trattoria-pizzeria with seafood
specialities. Closed Sunday
evening and Monday.*

Il Buco
via Sant'Ignazio 8
00186 Rome
Tel. 679 3298
*Tuscan specialities. Closed
Monday.*

Il Caminetto
viale dei Parioli 89
00197 Rome
Tel. 803946
*Closed Thursday. Outdoor
dining.*

Il Drappo
vicolo del Malpasso 9
00186 Rome
Tel. 687 7365
*Sardinian specialties.
Reservation essential. Closed
Sunday.*

Il Falchetto
via dei Montecatini 12/14
00186 Rome
Tel. 679 1160
*Country-style trattoria. Closed
Friday.*

La Sacrestia
via del Seminario 89
00186 Rome
Tel. 679 7581
*Typically decorated
pizzeria restaurant. Closed
Wednesday.*

La Scala
viale dei Parioli 79/d
00197 Rome
Tel. 808 3978
*Outdoor dining. Closed
Wednesday.*

La Toscana
via dei Crociferi 12
00187 Rome
Tel. 678 9971

Mario's Hostaria
piazza del Grillo 9
00184 Rome
Tel. 679 3725
Reserve. Closed Sunday.

Peppone
via Emilia 60
00187 Rome
Tel. 483976
Closed Sunday.

Piccolo Mondo
via Aurora 39/d
00187 Rome
Tel. 481 4595
*Elegant little taverna. Closed
Sunday.*

Piccola Roma
via Uffici del Vicario 36
00186 Rome
Tel. 679 8606
Closed Sunday.

Pierdonati
via della Conciliazione 39
00193 Rome
Tel. 654 3557
Closed Thursday.

Taverna Giulia
vicolo dell'Oro 23
00186 Rome
Tel. 686 9768
Ligurian specialities. Reservation essential. Closed Sunday.

Tempio di Bacco
via Lombardia 36/38
00187 Rome
Tel. 481 4625
Closed Saturday.

Tullio
via di San Nicola
da Tolentino 26
00187 Rome
Tel. 481 8564
Tuscan trattoria. Closed Sunday.

Vecchia Roma
piazza Campitelli 18
00186 Rome
Tel. 686 4604
*Seafood and Roman specialities.
Closed Wednesday.*

Outskirts of Rome

Cecilia Metella
via Appia Antica 125/127
00179 Rome
Tel. 513 6743
Outdoor dining. Closed Monday.

La Maielletta
via Aurelia Antica 270
00165 Rome
Tel. 637 7464
*Abruzzi specialities. Closed
Monday.*

Vecchia America
piazza Marconi 32
00144 Rome
Tel. 592 6601
*Typical restaurant and
"birreria", ale house. Closed
Tuesday.*

LOWER-PRICED
(below L. 40,000)

Cannavota
piazza San Giovanni
in Laterano 20
00184 Rome
Tel. 775007
Closed Wednesday.

Crisciotti-al Boschetto
via del Boschetto 30
00184 Rome
Tel. 474 4770
*Rustic trattoria. Outdoor dining.
Closed Saturday.*

Da Domenico
via di San Giovanni
in Laterano 134
00184 Rome
Tel. 734774
*Typical habitués' trattoria.
Closed Monday.*

Elettra
via Principe Amedeo 72
00185 Rome
Tel. 474 5397
*Typical habitués' trattoria.
Closed Friday evening and
Saturday.*

Grappolo d'Oro
via Palestro 4
00185 Rome
Tel. 494 1441
Closed Sunday.

Hostaria da Vincenzo
via Castelfidardo 6
00185 Rome
Tel. 484596
Closed Sunday.

La Buca di Ripetta
via di Ripetta 36
00186 Rome
Tel. 361 9391
*Typical habitués' trattoria.
Closed Sunday evening and
Monday.*

La Cabana
via del Mancino 7/9
00187 Rome
Tel. 679 1190
*Typical habitués' trattoria.
Closed Sunday.*

La Taverna
via Massimo d'Azeglio 3/f
00184 Rome
Tel. 474 4305
Closed Saturday.

La Tavernetta
via del Nazareno 3/4
00187 Rome
Tel. 679 3124
Closed Monday.

Mino
via Magenta 48
00185 Rome
Tel. 495 9202
Closed Saturday.

Monte Arci
via Castelfidardo 33
00185 Rome
Tel. 494 1347
*Trattoria with Sardinian
specialities. Closed Sunday.*

Taverna Trilussa
via del Politeama 23
00153 Rome
Tel. 581 8918
*Outdoor dining. Typical
establishment with Roman
specialities. Closed Sunday
evening and Monday.*

Outskirts of Rome

Da Giacobbe
via Appia Nuova 1681
00043 Ciampino
Tel. 724 0131
*Outdoor dining. Closed Monday.
Reservation essential.*

La Cuccagna
via Flaminia al km 16,500
00188 Rome
Tel. 691 2827
*Country restaurant with outdoor
dining and garden. Closed
Monday.*